MUSICAL GAMES AND ACTIVITIES

A Collection of Easy-to-Play Games and Activities for the Piano Studio or Music Classroom

This book contains an assortment of games and activities passed down from one teacher to another over the years, as well as fresh new ideas. All too often teachers collect music class activities with the belief that someday they will find the time to organize them for their studio or classroom. The author has done this for you. To make it easy for you, to apply them to your lesson plans, the games and activities are in categories with variations for other levels and home reinforcement suggestions.

Use these games and activities as a springboard to develop other creative ideas in your studio or classroom.

Compiled and written
by
Gloria Burnett Scott

Graphics by
Loren W. Gahnberg

TABLE OF CONTENTS

TWINS AND TRIPLETS RELAY RACE

Objective:	Help orient students to twins and triplets
Student level:	Very young beginners and Early Level I
Number of players:	At least two

Materials needed:
  - None

1. Group the students into two teams. Each team stands in a line at the right-hand end of each keyboard. The teacher stands at the left end of one keyboard and appoints someone to stand at the left end of the other. The teacher and the appointed person check that the students play correctly.

2. When the teacher says, "Go," the first student in each line plays all of the twins, striking both keys at the same time, from the high end down to the low end of the keyboard. Players can use both hands, striking two sets of twins at the same time.

3. The next student starts to play as soon as the first student has moved to the second or third set of twins. The team finishing first is the winner.

Next, the teacher asks the class to play all the triplets, using the same rules.

Variation:
Players strike the twins (or triplets) from the low end of the keyboard to the high end.

HOME REINFORCEMENT:
Assign daily practice to find and play all the twins and triplets.

KEYBOARD ORIENTATION

Objective:	Develop better sight-reading skills through the feel of the "Braille" on the piano keyboard
Student level:	Beginners of all ages
Number of players:	At least four

Materials needed:
- None

1. Four players face the keyboard. Players one and three close their eyes and try to find a group of twins, while players two and four observe.

2. Players two and four try to find a group of twins with their eyes closed, while players one and three watch.

3. The four players—continuing to alternate between the two pairs of players—try to find the triplets.

4. Then the teacher asks each pair of players to find, without looking, a twin group at the high end of the keyboard, then a triplet group at the bottom of the keyboard, the middle key of the triplet group, the bottom of a twin group, and so on.

5. Finally, with eyes open, each student reaches for the middle key of a triplet group and slides right onto the white key A, then plays B, and so on, until all seven letters of the musical alphabet have been played.

6. Now the teacher groups the students into two relay teams facing the keyboard. Each student quickly finds and plays A and goes to the end of the line. Then each one finds and plays B, and so on. Next, at the teacher's request, the students find and play: A-B-C, then C-D-E, E-F-G, A-B-A-G, and so on. Establish in the student's mind that, in the A-B-A-G configuration, G is easily found by going one step <u>down</u> the musical scale rather than six steps upward.

At some point during each lesson, ask the students to close their eyes and find A; then without opening their eyes, find C (by feeling it next to the bottom of the twins); next find F (by feeling it next to the bottom of the triplet grouping); and so on.

Mental Gymnastics: The teacher tells the class to face away from the piano with their eyes closed and to mentally picture the keyboard. He or she asks the class to give the name of the white key that is between the twins, then the name of the white key that is just above the triplet group, and so on.

HOME REINFORCEMENT:

1. Ask parents or other family members to quiz the student during the week, asking questions such as, "Which white key is just below the bottom of a triplet group?" The answer is "F."

2. Assign pupils to practice finding all the A's, B's, C's, and so forth, on the piano keyboard.

MUSICAL STAIRWAY

Objective:	Help orient students to "steps" and "skips"
Student level:	Very young beginners and Early Level I
Number of players:	Any number

Materials needed:
- A set of seven large cards (approximately 8" x 9") with one letter of the musical alphabet written on each card

1. The teacher arranges the lettered cards like a stairway on the floor, starting with A.

2. The students are shown that by walking from one letter to the next, they are "stepping." Each one takes a turn walking up and down the stairway, walking just above the cards rather than on them. The teacher explains that when they step over a letter, either up or down, they are "skipping."

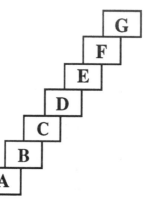

3. The teacher tells the first student to start on A, skip up, and step up, stopping right above the card. Then the teacher asks the class if the person landed on the correct stair. The student should be standing over the letter D.

4. The next person is directed to start on G and skip down twice, and so on.

Variation:
Group the students into two teams facing the keyboard. The first student in each line is asked to do an exercise similar to those explained above, only now on the keyboard.

For example, the first two students start on G and play the tone that is two skips down. They should quickly play C and rotate to the end of the line. The next two students start on D and play a skip and a step up. The activity continues until all players have had at least one turn. The class checks to see whether the students have played correctly.

HOME REINFORCEMENT:
Give students a list of skip-and-step activities to practice at home.

CLUES FOR STEPS AND SKIPS

Objective: Reinforce knowledge of steps and skips
Student level: Very young beginners and Early Level I
Number of players: Any number

Materials needed:
- A set of seven large cards (approximately 8" x 9") with one letter of the musical alphabet written on each card

1. Students are seated in a semicircle looking at the teacher. The teacher holds the stack of letter cards, with the letters facing away from the students.

2. The teacher selects a card and then gives the students a clue about it. For example, "I have a card that is a step above D. What is it?" The class answers, "E." The teacher shows the card, puts it in the back of the stack, and gives the next clue. "I have a card that is a skip down from B. What is it?" They answer, "G."

Variation:
In a week or two, give more complicated clues. For example, "I see a card that is two skips and a step up from E. What is it?" The class answers, "C."

HOME REINFORCEMENT:
1. Prepare a list of clues for parents to use to quiz students during the week.

2. Ask the students to prepare one or two clues to give to the class the following week.

MUSICAL ALPHABET TUNE-UP CARDS

Objective:	Visualize the arrangement of any five note tune-up grouping
Student level:	Very young beginners and Level I
Number of Players:	Five or more

Materials needed:
- A set of seven large cards (approximately 8" x 9") with one letter of the musical alphabet written on each card

1. All seven cards are dealt to the students. The teacher indicates where the person holding the card with the first letter of the five-note scale tune-up should stand. Students are then instructed to indicate accidentals on their five note tune-ups by either:

raising one arm in the air to represent a sharp, or

placing one hand on their shoulder to indicate a flat.

2. The teacher asks the students to quickly arrange themselves in the order of the "A Major" tune-up. They should arrange themselves as follows:

3. Using the keyboard, a classmate or the teacher plays the five-note scale arranged by the students. All listen, and if the students are in the correct order, the game continues with the teacher asking for another tune-up. The helpers help players to correct themselves in case of an error.

Variation:
Gather a large class into several groups and ask some students to be helpers. The helper's job is to check each group, making sure all players have arranged themselves in the correct order of the key called for by the instructor. Later, players can race to see which team can arrange themselves the fastest in the tune-up called for by the teacher.

HOME REINFORCEMENT:
On students' daily assignment sheets, assign singing or saying the letter names of the tune-up exercise. For example, in the key of D Major, the students sing, "D, E, F#, G, A, tunes-up in D."

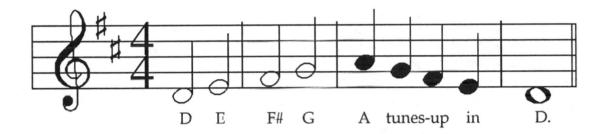

D   E   F#   G   A tunes-up in   D.

MAJOR TUNE-UP FLASH CARDS

Objective:	Visualize the arrangement of any five note tune-up grouping
Student level:	Very young beginners and Level I with variations for Level II and Level III
Number of Players:	Any number

Materials needed:
- Nine colored cards (made out of 8-1/2" x 11" construction paper or tag board, cut in half lengthwise—i.e., each card measures 4-1/4" x 11") for the teacher and a set of nine cards for each student
- 20 dark-colored and 25 light-colored 1" x 3" self-adhesive labels (available in stationery stores) for the teacher and a set of 20 dark-colored labels and 25 light-colored labels for each student

Arrange the labels, or strips, on each card to form a tune-up pattern for each major key. Write on the back of each card the name of the key the tune-up is in.

Key of D or A

Key of D-flat or A-flat

Key of E

Key of E-flat

Key of F

Key of F-sharp or G-flat

Key of B

Key of B-flat

Key of C or G

1. Each student is given nine cards, 25 light strips, and 20 dark strips. The teacher draws nine large rectangles on the board and writes underneath them the names of the major keys. Then the teacher asks the class to figure out the black and white patterns of the five tones for each tune-up pattern.

2. The teacher draws the first pattern in the rectangle on the board, and a student plays it on the piano. Then they all copy the pattern onto one of their cards and write the letter name of the key on the back. This activity continues until each member of the class has completed all nine tune-up cards.

3. The students are then shown the opposite relationships of the black and white patterns in D and D-flat, and are asked to match the other cards.

Key of D or A   Key of D-flat or A-flat   Key of E   Key of E-flat

4. The teacher groups the class as partners. The partners shuffle one set of tune-up cards and spread them face up on the table or floor. Each pair finds and groups the tune-up cards to show the opposite relationships of the keys.

Key of E   Key of E-flat

5. Arrange the students in a semicircle facing the teacher. The teacher shows a tune-up card and asks the class to tell the name of the key for that card.

6. A class seated at keyboards would say the name of the tune-up and then play it up and back. Ask the students to sing or say the black and white pattern of the tune-up as they play. For example, in the key of D, pupils sing, "white, white, black, white, white tunes-up in D."

White, white, black, white, white tunes-up   in   D.

Now repeat, singing or saying the letter names: "D, E, F-sharp, G, A tunes-up in D."

Variations:
1. Arrange students in a semicircle to play the "Around the World" game. (This game is a favorite activity.) The teacher shows a flash card to the first two students standing next to each other on the left and asks them to tell the name of the key for that card. (**Note:** *To encourage concentration, allow students only one answer for each play.*) The first one in the pair to get the correct answer takes the card and moves slightly behind the person on their left. The teacher shows the next card to these two players.

The winner always moves to the left and answers with the next student. If there is a tie, give both students a card—it doesn't matter which card—to add to their "holdings." Then show both students another flash card. Sometimes they will tie several times before one player can move on. Students try to win all the cards and make it all the way "around the world" to their original place in the semicircle. The student with the most cards wins.

2. Gather the class into two lines facing the teacher. The teacher shows a tune-up card to the first person in each line. Each player tries to say the name of the key before a player from the other team does. Give the card to the one who says the correct answer first. If there is a tie, the pair is shown another card. At the end of the game, a person from each team counts the cards their team has earned. The team with the most cards wins.

3. Students are seated in a semicircle. Toss a soft toy or bean bag to each person, asking each one to "spell" the black and white pattern on any key asked for. As soon as the student calls out the answer and tosses back the toy (or bag), play moves on to the next person. (This activity encourages pupils to think quickly on their feet.)

4. Play "Clue" with the students. The teacher holds a card and gives students a clue about the card. For example, "I see a card with white, black, black, white, white on it. What tune-up do I have?" The answer is "E."

5. *Level II and Level III:* Expand the flash cards to full major and minor scales, and use them with the activities outlined above.

HOME REINFORCEMENT:
Assign students daily practice in singing or saying each of their tune-up cards as they play them on the keyboard.

MYSTERY TUNE-UP

Objective:	Learn to "spell" the first five notes of each of the major scale tune-ups
Student level:	Very young beginners and Level I
Number of players:	Any number

Materials needed:
- Chalkboard or marker board

1. The students stand in a semicircle facing the board. The first student makes five short horizontal lines on the board. These lines represent the letters of the five note tune-up.

_____   _____   _____   _____   _____

2. The teacher asks one student to write the letter G over the second line, another student to write the letter A over the third line, and the next person to write the letter C over the fifth line.

_____   G   A   _____   C

3. The teacher asks a different student to fill in the two missing letters of the tune-up.

Answer: *F*   G   A   *Bb*   C

4. The teacher asks another person to come to the piano and play the tune-up notes, in order to check that the correct answer was given. Play continues until students have spelled all the tune-up patterns correctly.

Note: *Guide students to discover that they <u>cannot use two consecutive letters</u> that are the same. They must use a different letter over each line. In some cases ,they must apply an accidental to spell the tune-up correctly. For example, students mistakenly write an "E-flat tune-up" as E-flat, <u>F, F-sharp,</u> A-flat, B-flat, instead of E-flat, <u>F, G-flat,</u> A-flat, B-flat.*

Variation:
The teacher prepares a set of eighteen 2" x 3" letter cards and writes one of the following letters on each card: A, A-flat, A-sharp, B, B-flat, C, C-flat, C-sharp, D, D-flat, D-sharp, E, E-flat, F, F-sharp, G, G-flat, G-sharp. Then, the teacher shuffles the letter cards and all the cards are dealt to the class. Five pieces of 4" x 5" construction paper are arranged in a line on the floor. The teacher calls out the name of a tune-up. Students holding letter cards that spell the five tones quickly place them in the correct order on the 4" x 5" sheets. Then the teacher or a designated student plays the tune-up on the piano. Play continues as soon as the letter cards are placed correctly.

MAJOR TUNE-UP SPELLING

Objective:	Associate the black and white patterns with the letter names of the five note tune-up
Student level:	Very young beginners and Level I with variations for Mid-Level I and Level II
Number of players:	Four or more

Materials needed:
- A set of seven small cards (approximately 2" x 5") with one letter of the musical alphabet written on each card

- A set of 10 small cards with a flat on five of the cards and a sharp on the other five cards

- Five small black pieces and five small white pieces of construction paper

1. Group the class into two teams. Team 1 takes the five black and five white cards. Team 2 takes the letter cards and the accidentals When the instructor asks for the key of E, Team 1 arranges the black and white patterns in this order:

Team 2 places the correct letters and accidentals in the following pattern:

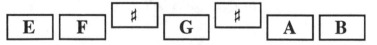

2. The two teams check each other to see whether the black and white patterns match the spelling of the tune-up. A student or the teacher plays the five-note scale arranged by the students. Through peer interaction, students help each other rearrange any incorrect cards.

Variations:
1. Use several sets of cards for large classes. Assign some students as helpers, to check that their group has arranged the cards correctly.

2. Group the class into two teams. When the teacher calls for the "E tune-up," the first student in Team 1 starts the pattern with a white piece of paper. The second student finds a black one and puts it next to the white one, and so on.

Team 2 puts down the first letter of the tune-up. The second student places the next letter and accidental to the right of the first, and so on. The activity continues until the black and white pattern and all letters and accidentals of the tune-up are in the correct position. The last two students go to the keyboard and play what the two groups have arranged.

3. *Mid-Level I and Level II:* Expand cards to an entire major or minor scale.

A	B	C	D	E	F	G
♭	♭	♭	♭	♭	♭	♭
♯	♯	♯	♯	♯	♯	♯

FIVE NOTE TUNE-UP FLASH CARDS

Objective:	Further develop quick recognition of the first five notes of a major scale
Student level:	Very young beginners and Level I with variations for Late Level I, Level II and Level III
Number of Players:	Four or more

Materials needed:
- A set of Chromatic flash cards separated into two piles, with all treble clef cards in one pile and all bass clef cards in the other

1. The teacher groups the class into two teams (two to six on a team). All the treble clef cards are spread face-up on the floor in front of one team, and all the bass clef cards are spread face-up in front of the other team.

2. The teacher calls out a key and asks the students in each team to arrange the cards in the order of the five note tune-up. For example, players with bass clef cards would arrange the key of B Major like this:

3. The teacher or a student goes to the keyboard and plays the five-note scale the two teams have arranged. Through peer interaction, the players help one another correct errors.

Note: *For larger classes and more teams, use several decks of cards.*

Variations:
1. Turn this activity into a relay race. The first student on each team finds the first note of the tune-up. The second student finds the second note and places it next to the first one, and so on. The first team to finish with all the notes in the correct order is the winner.

2. *Late Level I, Level II and Level III:* Expand this game so that students arrange full major and minor scales.

HOME REINFORCEMENT:
Strengthen students' skills with an assignment of daily practice using their Chromatic flash cards to find the notes for each five note tune-up.

RELATING THE GRAND STAFF AND KEYBOARD

Objective:	Develop a functional process of note recognition to increase reading skills rather than to learn jingles that complicate music reading.
Student level:	Very young beginners and Level I
Number of players:	Any number

Materials needed:
- One set each of Lines and Spaces flash cards and Chromatic flash cards
- Bean bag
- Four 2" x 2" pieces of construction paper
- Chalkboard or marker board with staff lines
- Flannel board
- Floor staff or floor keyboard

DIVIDING THE PIANO KEYBOARD

1. On the piano keyboard, place the 2" x 2" cards between the keys G and A in the two octaves above and below middle C.

The cards will act as "fences" to isolate the three groupings of the musical alphabet and to aid students in playing notes in the correct octaves.

2. On the music rack of the piano, place a chart of the piano keyboard and the Grand Staff, both divided into three sections, like the graphic example on the next page.

Help students see the three groupings of the musical alphabet in the center of the piano keyboard. Point out that each note has a particular place on the keyboard. For instance, if the flash card shows "first space A" in the bass clef, the students should look at the Grand Staff (see figure below) and find "first space A." Students can then find "first space A" between the first two dividers placed on the piano keyboard and play the correct note.

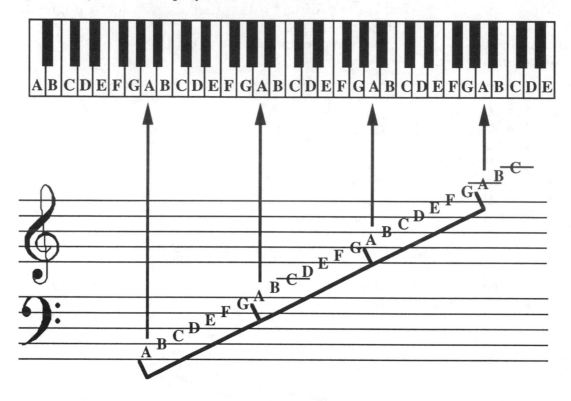

3. Group the students into two lines facing the keyboard. The teacher places flash cards on the music rack. If the first card shown is "Treble Clef second space," the first two students in each line help each other by referring to the figure (above) to find where that note is on the Grand Staff. Then they check to see which grouping of the musical alphabet on the keyboard it falls within. "Treble Clef second space" is Treble Clef A, and it falls in the third grouping of the musical alphabet. Students slide their card behind the correct piano key in the third "fenced off" section on the piano so that the note is directly behind the corresponding key.

4. After the other members of the class check that it is placed correctly, remove the flash card. Play continues until all students have had at least one turn. In the beginning, to facilitate peer interaction, have students work together rather than competing against one another in teams.

After a few weeks of this activity, let the students in each line race to play on the keyboard the note shown on the flash card. The note must be played in the correct octave. The winner takes the card, and both students rotate to the end of their respective lines.

When most students are able to find the correct places for the various notes, continue the activity without the "fences".

HOME REINFORCEMENT - at the Keyboard:
Assign the above-mentioned activity for daily practice at home until students are competent in finding the correct placement of notes on the keyboard.

WRITING REINFORCEMENT AT THE BOARD

1. The teacher writes the names of the musical alphabet on the lines and spaces of the Grand Staff, starting with "bass clef first space A" and ending with G. Point out that each letter moves from a space to a line as it steps upward. Put a bracket under these first seven letters, and write the next two groups above the bracket, as shown below.

Often students write too many letters in the large area between the bass and treble clefs. Show the class that even though there is a large open space, the letters still only move from space to line, and only three letters fill the space between the bass and treble clefs.

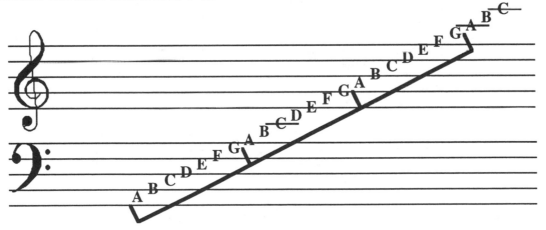

2. Group the class into pairs to work together at the board. One student writes the names of the lines and spaces; the other student helps. Then switch, so all players get a chance to write. Some partners could be working on a flannel board while others lay out cards with letters on them on a floor keyboard.

3. Point out that the musical alphabet grouping that starts on "treble clef second space" is always one space higher than the same letter in the grouping that starts on "bass clef first space."

4. Students face the board and watch as the teacher points to the lines and spaces, asking pupils to call out the name of the line or space as he or she points to it.

Variations:
1. Group the class into two teams facing the chalkboard or marker board for a relay race. When the teacher says, "Start," the team captains draw a treble clef and a bass clef and write the letter A in the first space of the base clef.

Then the students quickly pass their chalk (or marker) to the next player on their team, who fills in the letter B. The game continues until students have written the musical alphabet in all three places on the Grand Staff. The team that finishes first has their work checked by the other team.

2. With two teams facing the board, ask the first player on each team to write four B's in their respective places on the Grand Staff. Ask the next players to write five C's, and so forth.

3. The teacher calls out a word that uses letters only from the musical alphabet. The students write the word on the Grand Staff, placing the letters on the correct lines and spaces in the treble and bass clefs (ACE, FEED, EDGE, CAGE, and so on.). To assist the early speller, write the words on cards, and set them on the chalk (or marker) tray.

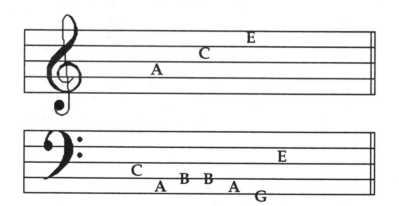

FLASH CARD REINFORCEMENT

In introducing the Chromatic flash cards or the Lines and Spaces flash cards (whichever you are using), start with only three cards in the bass clef and three in the treble clef. Before class, take out the following six notes from the Lines and Spaces flash cards: bass clef "first space A" through "second space C" (three cards), and treble clef "second space A" through "third space C" (three cards).

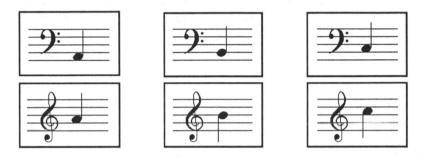

Note: *Private studio teachers will have more success if students have their own sets of flash cards for daily use. In advance of the class, take out the six cards mentioned above. Each week, add a few more cards until the students have learned the whole set of cards. Public School teachers may want to have on hand some sets for students to borrow.*

2. Teach students to read the cards from left to right, saying "treble clef second space A" or "bass clef third line D," and so on, for the first three or four weeks. Students often see only the note, ignoring the clef sign on the flash card.

3. Group the students into two teams facing the piano. Place one of the six flash cards on the music rack. Ask the first two students to play the note on the card in its correct place on the piano. The remaining students check to see which student plays the correct note first. That student takes the card, and both students rotate to the end of the line. If both students play the correct note, they each take a card and move to the end of the line.

Add a few cards each week as students become competent.

Eventually remove the little 2" x 2" card fences and continue playing the game until the students are well grounded.

HOME REINFORCEMENT - Flash Cards:
Students place the stack of flash cards on the music rack of their piano and play the note on the first card. A parent or other member of the family can check that the note was played in the correct place on the keyboard. Continue until the student has played all cards correctly. The players may want to set a timer to see how quickly they can go through the stack of cards. Each day as they practice this activity, they should try to beat the time it took to go through the cards during the previous practice.

REINFORCEMENT THROUGH MENTAL GYMNASTICS

1. Arrange the students in a semicircle. The teacher tosses a bean bag to the first person at the left end of the semicircle and asks the name of "bass clef second line." The student replies "B," and throws the bean bag back to the teacher. The teacher then tosses the bean bag to the next player and asks a similar question.

2. Instruct students to quickly toss the bean bag back to the teacher after they give the answer. A person who does not know the answer tosses the bean bag right back to the teacher. The teacher then tosses the bean bag to the next player and asks the same question. This keeps the students thinking while others are answering.

As you assign additional flash cards, use them in your mental gymnastics activity.

HOME REINFORCEMENT - Mental Gymnastics:
Send home a list of mental gymnastics questions about lines and spaces. Parents can quiz the students while they are riding in a car or helping with chores at home.

HAND STAFF

Objective:	Reinforce the learning of the lines and spaces on the Grand Staff
Student level:	Very young beginners and Level I
Number of players:	Any number

Materials needed:
- A set of Lines and Spaces flash cards

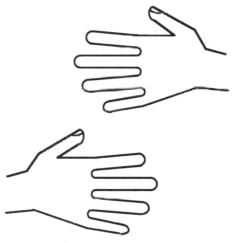

1. Instruct students to look at the palms of their hands, with the thumbs upward and fingers slightly spread. The right hand should be above the left, as shown. Each finger symbolizes a line of the staff, and each hand symbolizes one of the clefs.

2. Have the students mentally number their fingers, starting with the little finger which represents line one on the staff. Then have them number the four spaces between the fingers, which represent the spaces on the staff.

Note: *When instructing young children , have each child take their left hand and grab each of the fingers on their right hand as they number them . Reverse the action for the left hand.*

3. Ask students to locate treble space A on their hand staffs. Using their left hands, students point to the second space on their right hands. Now find and name a skip up from A. Repeat the activity to reinforce the lines and spaces in the bass clef, which are on the left hand.

4. Use the hand staff to drill students on skips, steps, and intervals.

Variation:
Hold a set of Lines and Spaces flash cards facing away from the students and tell the students the clef sign and name of the line or space shown on the card. Students show the answer on their hand staffs The instructor then shows the student the card, so they can check whether they have pointed to the correct line or space.

HOME REINFORCEMENT:
Show parents how they can help students by practicing the variation with them at home.

SCRAMBLED ALPHABET

Objective:	Further develop quick recognition of the names of the lines and spaces
Student level:	Very young beginners and Level I
Number of players:	Two or more

Materials needed:
* A set of Lines and Spaces flash cards with the answers on the back blocked out with felt pen or stickers

1. Spread the Lines and Spaces flash cards face up on the floor.

2. Group the class into two or more teams facing the cards. If the class is large and there are several teams, choose a helper for each team. An extra player can help the teacher check the cards picked up by the students.

3. The teacher calls out a note, and the first player in each line rushes to the flash cards to see how many they can find with the correct note on it. They bring their cards to the teacher or team helper to check. Set a time limit by having players who are waiting for their turn slowly count aloud together. For example, at the count of 10, players looking for cards must stop and show the cards they have found. Any incorrect cards are returned to the floor. Players keep the correct cards and rotate to the end of the line. The game continues until all the cards are picked up.

4. The player in the front of each line collects and counts the cards for the team .

Variation:
Make a set of 14 small cards. Write on each card one letter of the musical alphabet and a treble clef or a bass clef sign, as shown below. Each team will need a set of cards. Shuffle each set, and place one face down in front of each team.

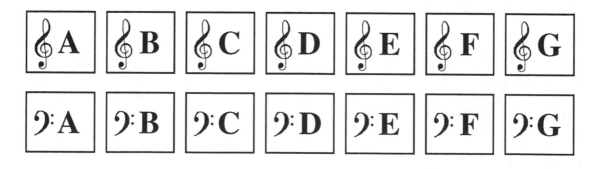

The first member of each team draws a letter from the top of the pile and must quickly find a matching note card on the floor. For example, if Team 1 draws the letter "treble clef F," the student must quickly find an F-note card in treble clef on the floor. The first team to find all the correct notes wins.

HOME REINFORCEMENT:
Cut a set of 14 small cards for each student. Have the students write one letter of the musical alphabet in treble clef on one card and in bass clef on another card. At home, assign students to spread out their Lines and Spaces flash cards on the floor and to place their fourteen small cards face down in a stack. They draw a card from this stack and then search for the matching flash card on the floor.

AROUND THE WORLD

Objective:	Further motivate students to learn the names of lines and spaces
Student level:	Very young beginners and Level I
Number of players:	Four or more

Materials needed:
- A set of Chromatic flash cards or Lines and Spaces flash cards

1. Students stand in a semicircle facing the teacher.

2. The teacher shows a flash card, pulled from the back of the stack, to the first two students standing next to each other on the left. The students are asked to tell the name of the note. To encourage concentration, allow students only one answer.

3. The first student in the pair to get the correct answer takes the card and moves slightly behind the person on their left. The teacher shows the next card to these two players.

4. The winner moves to the left and answers with the next player in the semicircle. If there is a tie, give both students a card—it doesn't matter which card—to add to their "holdings." Then show another flash card to this pair. Sometimes they will tie several times before one player can move on.

5. Students try to win all the cards and make it all the way "around the world" to their original place in the semicircle. The student with the most cards wins.

HOME REINFORCEMENT:
The students make a game of working through the stack of Lines and Spaces flash cards each day. They say the name of the note seen on each card and immediately turn the card over to see if the answer is correct. All correct cards are placed in one pile and any wrong cards are placed in another pile. After going through all the cards, the student reworks the collection of wrong ones. Later in the week, suggest that students set a timer to see how fast they can say all the notes in the set of flash cards correctly. Assign this activity for several weeks as they gain accuracy and speed in identifying the names of the lines and spaces.

WORD SPELL

Objective:	Strengthen student's ability to recognize the names of the lines and spaces of the Grand Staff
Student level:	Very young beginners and Level I
Number of players:	Two or more

Materials needed:
- Construction paper or cardboard with musical words that use only the seven letters of the musical alphabet written on each piece
- A set of Lines and Spaces flash cards with the answers on the back blocked out with felt pen or stickers

1. Group the class into pairs. Give each pair a word card with a word of the same length on each card. If there are only two players, give each player a word card. The pairs put the word cards on the floor in front of them. Spread the set of Lines and Spaces flash cards face up on the floor in easy reach of the players. The teacher decides if the pairs will pick up flash cards in only the treble clef, just the bass clef, or a mixture of treble and bass clef cards to spell their words.

2. When the teacher says, "Start," each set of partners tries to find the flash cards that spell their word and places these flash cards above their word card, as shown below.

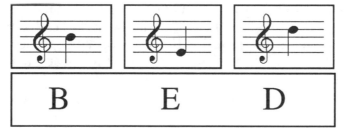

3. As soon as all the partners have found the notes that spell their word, ask them to check to see whether the partners next to them have spelled their word correctly. You may want to have the students play their words on the piano.

HOME REINFORCEMENT:
Cut six 4" x 8" pieces of construction paper for each student. The teacher writes six musical words on the board. Students copy them onto their construction paper. Assign daily work finding the notes in their sets of flash cards that match the words. One day, have students find only notes in the bass clef. The next day, look for notes in treble clef; then, a mixture of bass and treble clefs.

WHAT IS IT?

Objective:	Visualize the letter names of the lines and spaces
Student level:	Very young beginners and Level I
Number of players:	Any number

Materials needed:
- A set of Chromatic flash cards or Lines and Spaces flash cards

1. The class stands in a semicircle facing the teacher. The teacher holds the flash cards in such a way that players cannot see the answers.

2. The teacher gives the players a clue about the flash card. For example, "I have a card that shows a note on treble clef fourth space. What is it?" The answer is "E." "I have a card that has a note with a flat beside it on bass clef second line. What is it?" The answer is "B-flat."

3. Hand the card to the first player who gives the correct answer.

Variation:
Level I: Group the students into two teams facing the teacher. The teacher gives the clue to the first player on Team 1. The student answering correctly takes the card and moves to the end of the line. Give a clue for the next card to the student on Team 2. A player who gives the wrong answer moves to the end of the line. The teacher then repeats the clue for the next player on the other team. This continues until someone gives the right answer. Limit each team member to one answer for each turn.

MUSICAL TIC-TAC-TOE

Objective:	Further develop skills in recognizing the names of lines and spaces, notes, rests, and other musical terminology
Student level:	Very young beginners and Level I
Number of players:	At least four players

Materials needed:
- Chalkboard or marker board with three sets of staff lines drawn on the board
- A set of Lines and Spaces flash cards

1. Group the players into two teams called the "Treble Clefs" and the "Bass Clefs," with the students facing towards the chalkboard or marker board.

2. Draw a tic-tac-toe matrix over the three sets of staff lines on the board, and write the letter name of a line or space at the top of each square.

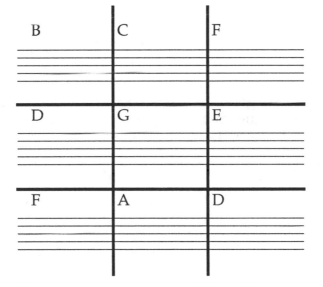

3. The Treble Clef team begins. The first player chooses a tic-tac-toe strategy as well as the note the team will start with. If the center square is chosen (shown above as G), the student draws a treble clef, to show that the Treble Clef team occupies that square, and then writes a whole note either on treble clef line G or treble clef space G above the staff.

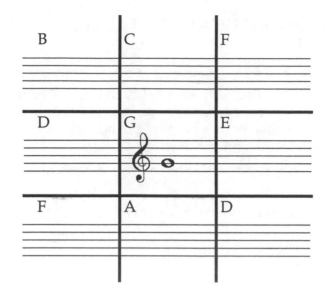

4. The other team watches and discusses the answer. If they decide that the Treble Clef team has written the note correctly, play continues. If the answer is written incorrectly, they erase both the incorrect note and the treble clef sign, and that square is again open to play. The next player, on the Bass Clef team, moves to the board and chooses an empty square in which to write his or her clef sign and a whole note, and so forth.

5. As in a regular tic-tac-toe game, the team that gets three of the same clef signs in a row is the winner.

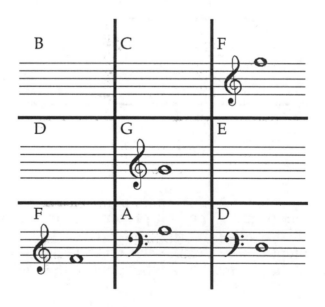

Variations:

1. Write in each of the squares the time values of notes and rests (see diagram below). Ask students to draw the correct note or rest when it is their turn to play. As before, the team with three clef signs in a row is the winner.

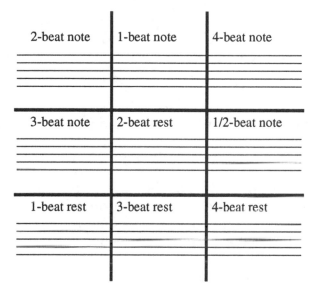

2-beat note	1-beat note	4-beat note
3-beat note	2-beat rest	1/2-beat note
1-beat rest	3-beat rest	4-beat rest

2. Write the names of musical symbols in each square. Instruct teams to draw the correct symbol in the squares they choose.

forte	repeat sign	mezzo-forte
mezzo-piano	decrescendo	accent
crescendo	piano	fermata

For other variations on musical Tic-Tac-Toe, see chapter 4 on key signatures and chapter 6 on triads.

THINK

Objective:	Test the student's ability to recognize and correctly name lines and spaces
Student level:	Very young beginners and Level I with variations for Late Level I, Level II and Level III.
Number of players:	Three or more

Materials needed:
- A set of Chromatic flash cards or Lines and Spaces flash cards

1. Students stand in a line or semicircle facing the teacher.

2. The teacher pulls a flash card from the back of the stack and shows it to the first student at the left end of the line. The student is allowed only one answer. Set a time limit for responding (such as 5-10 slow taps of the foot). The teacher keeps the card when the player answers correctly. If the answer is incorrect, the teacher hands the card to the student and says, "THINK!" The pupil studies the flash card and keeps it until the game is over. The teacher moves on to show the next person a card.

3. When the game ends, quiz the students on the cards they missed. The player with the smallest number of flash cards is the winner.

Variations:
Late Level I: Play the game, substituting Major Triads flash cards and/or Minor Triads flash cards or Key Signature flash cards instead of Lines and Spaces flash cards.

Level II: Use Diminished Triads flash cards.

Level III: Use Augmented Triads flash cards.

HOME REINFORCEMENT:
Prior to playing Think, assign daily review of the flash cards you will be using for the game. Instruct students to make a game of working through the stack of flash cards every day. They say the name of the note on the card and immediately turn the card over to see whether they answered correctly. Place all the cards for which the correct answer was given in one stack, and place all the other cards in another stack. After going through all the cards, the student reworks the collection for which wrong answers were given. Later in the week, suggest that players set a timer to see how fast they can say all the notes in the set of flash cards correctly. Assign this activity for several weeks until students gain speed in identifying the names of the lines and spaces.

READING MUSICAL WORDS

Objective:	Sharpen the student's skills in recognizing the names of the lines and spaces
Student level:	Late Level I and Level II
Number of players:	Any number

Materials needed:
- Several large cards (approximately 5" x 10") made from heavy paper, with words using the musical alphabet written on them
- A buzzer or a call bell

Using heavy paper, cut the 5" x 10" cards. Draw the five staff lines and a clef sign on each card, and write a word in whole notes, using only the letters from the musical alphabet, on each card. (See examples below.)

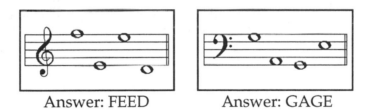

Answer: FEED   Answer: GAGE

1. Group the class into two teams facing a table or piano bench, with a buzzer or call bell within easy reach of both teams.

2. Show a card to the first player in each line. The first player to recognize the word on the card presses the buzzer and gives the answer. The student giving the correct answer takes the word card and both players rotate to the end of the line. If the first player answers incorrectly, the other player answers. The game continues with the next two players in line. The team with the most cards wins.

Variations:
1. The class sits in a semicircle facing the teacher. The teacher shows the flash card to the class. The first student to call out the right answer takes the card, goes to the keyboard, and plays the word. This player remains by the piano and checks whether the other students play their words correctly. Play continues until all students have answered and played their words.

2. Play "Around The World" using these flash cards. (See game rules earlier in this chapter.)

GRAND STAFF UPSET

Objective:	Reinforce the student's ability to quickly recall the names of the lines and spaces on the Grand Staff
Student level:	Late Level I and Level II
Number of players:	Six or more

Materials needed:
- Two sets of seven small cards (approximately 2" x 3") with one letter of the musical alphabet written on each card

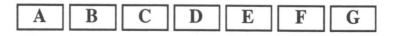

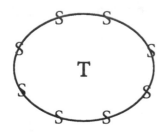

Note: *You will need a large area to play this game.*

1. The players stand in a large circle, and the teacher distributes all the cards to them. The teacher is "It" and stands in the middle of the circle. Players check their cards to make sure they do not have two cards with letters alike. If anyone does, the teacher takes one and switches it with a card from another player.

2. The teacher starts the game by calling out a given line or space on the Grand Staff. If the teacher calls out, "bass clef first space," the two students who have the cards with the letter A on them look at the students around the circle, secretly signaling that they have the cards. When the two students with the A cards make eye contact, they step forward and try to quickly exchange places before the teacher can get into one of their places. If the teacher gets into one of their spots before the two students exchange places, the student without a place becomes "It." The teacher takes the student's cards and stands with the other players in the circle.

3. Sometimes a student holds the letter called for but has forgotten the name of a line or space and does not move. The player holding the matching card steps forward, looking around for someone to exchange places with. At this point, the teacher asks who has the matching card. The player who held the identical card but did not change places becomes "It." The student who was "It" now takes that player's cards and returns to the circle.

4. Occasionally call, "Grand Staff Upset." All students in the circle quickly exchange places. "It" attempts to get into any other player's place and force that player into the center of the circle. The player in the center is now "It."

Since this game takes longer to play than some of the other games, you may wish to save it for special occasions.

For other variations on this game, see the chapter 4 on key signatures and chapter 6 on triads.

BASEBALL

Objective:	Motivate students to learn and practice the names of the lines and spaces
Student level:	Late Level I and Level II with variations for Late Level I and Level II
Number of players:	At least six players

Materials needed:
- A set of Chromatic flash cards or Lines and Spaces flash cards

Note: *A large playing area (approximately 10' x 12') is recommended.*

1. Group students into two teams and ask them to choose team names. Instruct the first team to quickly line up directly behind the teacher, at home plate. The first team is the offensive team—the team at bat.

2. The teacher then moves into position as the pitcher and assigns the remaining students to defensive positions in the infield (first base player, second base player, third base player, and catcher) and a score keeper at the board. The catcher stands to the right of the batter.

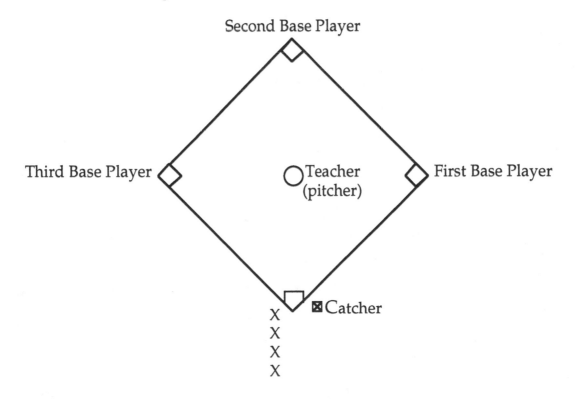

Note: *With a larger class, in order to involve all the students, set up two lines facing the pitcher. One line is the team at bat; the other line is a team of rotating catchers. There can also be an umpire. For a smaller number of students, set up fewer bases.*

3. The pitcher shows the Lines and Spaces flash card to the batter and to the catcher. If the catcher gives the answer first, the batter is out and goes to the end of the line. The score keeper marks down the out. However, if the batter says the answer first, the batter moves to first base. A tie goes to the runner. Any team member already on first base moves to second base.

4. To keep runners and infielders alert, the pitcher may turn around suddenly and show a flash card to two players standing at the same base. In order to stay on base, the runner must give the answer before the base player does. If the base player says the answer first, the runner is out and returns to the line behind home plate. The score keeper tallies the out. Allow teams only three outs per inning.

5. Quickly move the offensive team to their new defensive positions in the infield. The former infielders now take their place in line at home plate.

Note: *To prevent the game from getting too wild, eliminate base stealing, and keep all the rules as simple as possible.*

Variations:

Lines and Spaces Baseball
Late Level I and Level II: Instead of showing flash cards, ask students the name for "treble clef fifth line," or "bass clef third space," and so on.

Key Signature Baseball
Level I: Play Key Signature Baseball by substituting the Lines and Spaces flash cards with Key Signature flash cards and use the same rules as above.

Level II: Instead of showing flash cards to the student, tell the batter and catcher that you see a major key signature with four sharps on it. Ask them to give you the answer (E Major).

Triad Baseball
Level I: Using the above rules, substitute Major Triads or Minor Triads flash cards. Try mixing Major Triads and Minor Triads flash cards together.

Level II: Review with Major and Minor Triads flash cards and add Diminished Triads flash cards.

Level III: Show Key Signature flash cards and ask students to spell a major, minor, diminished, or augmented triad in first or second inversion. Another week, play Baseball using Augmented Triads flash cards. Then mix sets of Major, Minor, Diminished and Augmented Triads together.

Level IV or Level V: Show a Major, Minor, or Diminished Triads flash card and ask students to give the name of the note that will be the top of a major, dominant, minor, half diminished seventh, or full diminished seventh chord.

HOME REINFORCEMENT:
Assign daily review of the flash cards the week before you plan to play the Baseball game. Instruct students to make a game of working through the stack of flash cards every day. They say the name of the note on the card and immediately turn the card over to see if they answered correctly. Place all the cards for which the correct answer was given in one stack, and place all the other cards in another stack. After going through all the cards, the student reworks the collection for which wrong answers were given. Later in the week, suggest that students set a timer to see how fast they can say all the notes in the set of flash cards correctly. Assign this activity for several weeks until students gain speed in identifying the names of the lines and spaces.

KEY SIGNATURE PATTERNS

Objective:	Simplify the learning of the sharp and flat patterns
Student level:	Very young beginners and Early Level I with variations for Mid-Level I and Late Level I
Number of players:	At least seven

Materials needed:
- A large floor staff or five strings arranged on the floor to represent the five lines on the staff
- A set of seven large cards (approximately 8" x 9") with one letter of the musical alphabet written on each card

1. The teacher gives one card to each student. If necessary, the teacher can play the game, too. Players hold the letter cards in front of them with the letters facing outward.

2. The teacher demonstrates to each player their correct position on the floor staff. If they have the letter B, they stand on treble clef third line. When the teacher says "flats," the players see how quickly they can arrange themselves in the correct pattern for flats on the floor staff.

3. The remaining students check to see that players are in the right order and help adjust students who need correcting. Play continues with the calling of "sharps."

Variation:
Mid- to Late Level I: Each player holds a card facing outward. The teacher calls a key signature in either treble or bass clef. Players holding the letter cards for that key signature arrange themselves in the proper order on the floor staff. For example, the teacher calls, "Key of E-flat in treble clef." Students holding cards with the letters B, E, and A dash to the floor keyboard and stand on the lines and spaces for that key. The players' peers check to see that they are standing in the correct position.

HOME REINFORCEMENT:
Assign daily practice in saying the letter names in the order of flats and sharps as they appear on the Grand Staff.

DOUBLE DICE GAME

Objective:	Aid in the learning of key signatures
Student level:	Very young beginners and Level I
Number of players:	Any number of students

Materials needed:
* Two blank dice

Mark three sides of the first die with a sharp sign. Mark the other three sides with a flat sign. Mark the other die with the numbers "1" through "6."

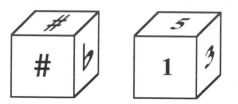

Students sit in a semicircle. The teacher rolls the two dice toward the first student on the left. If the first die comes up with a "sharp" and the other die has a "3," the student has to say the first three sharps in order (F-sharp, C-sharp, G-sharp). If the student answers incorrectly, the teacher calls on the next student in the semicircle. Play continues until all students have had at least one turn.

Variations:

1. Group students into two teams facing the board. The teacher rolls the dice beside them, on a table or piano bench. If one die shows a "flat" and the other die, a "5," the first two students on each team race to the board and write the name of the key (D-flat) and the five flats in the correct order.

2. Students may also respond by saying the names of the sharps or flats, in order, and the key signature that correspond to the number shown on the two dice.

HOME REINFORCEMENT:
Direct students to play this game at home by using a die from one of their games. Before throwing the die, the player decides if he or she wants to answer with sharps or flats. The player throws the die and quickly says the names of the sharps or flats and the key signature that correspond to the number shown on the die. The pupils check their answers with the aid of a key signature chart.

CHEER FOR THE FLATS AND SHARPS!

Objective:	Teach the shape of the flat and sharp patterns
Student level:	Very young beginners and Early Level I
Number of players:	Any number

Materials needed:
- None

1. The teacher reviews the placement of the flat pattern with the students by asking them to stand and tell where the flats are on the staff. The students first answer is, "Treble clef third line." The teacher tells them to imagine they have a Grand Staff in front of them and to put the sides of their right hands on the third line to show where the first flat is placed.

2. The teacher then asks them to verbalize and shape the next flat. The students answer, "Treble clef fourth space," and move their hands up to where they think the fourth space would be. Continue to review and shape the flat pattern.

3. The class continues standing, facing the teacher. The teacher acts as a cheerleader for the Flat team. The teacher starts the cheer by saying, "Give me a B," and shaping it in the air. With enthusiasm, the students say, "B," and shape it in the air as though they were touching an invisible staff. The teacher then says, "Give me an E," again shaping it in the air. The students say, "E," and shape it in front of them. The cheer continues, with students responding for the remaining flats.

4. Repeat the activity for the sharp pattern.

HOME REINFORCEMENT:
Assign one or two students to practice being cheerleaders so they can lead the class the next time they meet. To save time, one student leads the cheer for the Flat team and the other student leads the cheer for the Sharp team. Continue this activity over a number of weeks until all students have had a chance to lead the class.

KEY SIGNATURE DICE GAME

Objective:	Simplify the learning of key signatures
Student level:	Level I with variations for Late Level I and Level II
Number of players:	Any number

Materials needed:
- One regular die
- A chart showing the flats and sharps in each major key signature

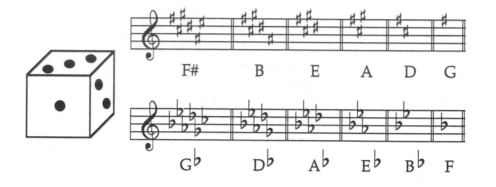

1. Players and teacher are seated on the floor in a circle or stand around a table with the chart showing how many flats or sharps are in each major key signature.

2. The teacher starts the play by calling either flats or sharps and rolls the die into the middle of the circle. If the die shows a three and the teacher has called for flats, the players look at the chart to find the key signature with three flats. Players also look for the name of the key. The first player to answer, "E-flat," is handed the die. This player rolls the die, remembering to ask for either flats or sharps before rolling.

3. Play continues until the entire class has had at least one turn.

Note: *When the class is able to answer more quickly, ask how many can play without the aid of the chart. When the students no longer need their charts, it will be hard for the teacher to decide who gave the correct answer first. When that happens, roll the die to each student separately, and ask that student to respond.*

Variations:
Late Level I and Level II: Roll the die and ask students to give the relative minor key signature. Later, request that they answer with the names of both the major and relative minor keys.

HOME REINFORCEMENT:
Encourage students to play this game at home during the week, either by themselves or with family members.

KEY SIGNATURE EAR TRAINING

Objective:	Reinforce key signatures and at the same time develop an ability to hear intervals in music
Student level:	Level I
Number of players:	Any number

Materials needed:
- Chalkboard or marker board
- Key Signature flash cards
- Floor staff
- A set of seven large cards (approximately 8" x 9") with one letter of the musical alphabet written on each card

1. The teacher prepares the seven letter cards and gives one to each player.

2. Students listen to and shape the intervals in the air with their finger as the instructor plays the first six flats on the piano, as follows: starting with B-flat, going up to E-flat, down to A-flat, up to D-flat, down to G-flat, and up to C-flat. The class recognizes these intervals as the flat pattern.

3. The teacher reviews the sharp patterns, playing the first six sharps, as follows: starting with F sharp, going down to C-sharp, up to G-sharp, down to D-sharp, down to A-sharp, and up to E-sharp.

4. The teacher plays the sharps or flats in one of the key signatures on the piano. For example, for the key of A-flat, the teacher plays the first four flats of the key signature, as follows: starting with B-flat, going up to E-flat, down to A-flat, and up to D-flat. Students holding the letter cards that match these notes quickly arrange themselves on the floor staff in the pattern of the key signature they just heard. Players hold their card in front of them so the rest of the class can check that they are standing in the correct place.

Key of A-Flat

To indicate that they are sharps, students raise one hand in the air. To indicate flats, they put one hand on their shoulder, as shown below.

Sharp   Flat

Variations:
1. The teacher spreads a set of Key Signature flash cards on the floor, and the players form a circle around the cards. The teacher plays a key signature pattern on the piano. Players listen and then quickly try to find the correct Key Signature card.

2. The students step to the board in pairs. The teacher asks one person to write and the other student to help. The teacher will play the sharps or flats of a key signature on the piano, and the students will write the key signature pattern on the board. For example, the teacher plays the first three sharps of the sharp key signature, and the students write the A-Major key signature pattern on the board. The helpers check and make any needed corrections. Helpers switch roles with writers and listen to the next key signature the teacher plays.

HOME REINFORCEMENT:
Students place their Key Signature flash cards face up on the music rack of the piano. They play the sharps or flats in the order shown on each card. The D-Major key signature, shown in bass clef, would be played from F-sharp down to C-sharp, in the octave below middle C.

KEY SIGNATURE AND MATCHING NOTE RELAY

Objective:	Strengthen the recognition of key signatures
Student level:	Level I and Level II with variations for Late Level I and Level II
Number of players:	Six or more

Materials needed:
- A set of Chromatic flash cards
- A set of Key Signature flash cards

1. Prior to class, remove approximately 12 (the number is optional) Chromatic flash cards and match them with the Key Signature flash cards of the same name.

2. Group the students into two teams. Spread the Key Signature flash cards, face up, on the floor in one area and the Chromatic Lines and Spaces flash cards, face up, in another area. One student on each team will act as a checker for the team.

3. The first student in each line picks up a Chromatic card from the floor and passes it quickly to the next player on the team. That player must look for a matching Key Signature card. For example, if the note on the Chromatic card is B, the student must look for the B-Major Key Signature card. As soon as the student finds the matching Key Signature card, he or she shows both cards to the team checker. Students with correct cards keep them; students with incorrect cards put them back on the floor. Then these players each pick up a Chromatic card, pass it to the next teammate in line, and move to the end of the line. The game continues until students have found all the matching cards.

Variations:
Mix together the Key Signature and the Chromatic cards, and spread them face up on the floor. The first player in each line picks a Chromatic card and finds the matching major Key Signature card. Players show their selected cards to the designated checker. If they picked the correct matching cards, the players keep the cards and move to the end of the line. If a players does not pick matching cards, the teacher places the incorrect cards back on the floor and the player moves to the back of the line. The teams count their cards at the end of the game.

Late Level I and Level II: Ask students to select a note and then find the minor Key Signature card with the same name.

HOME REINFORCEMENT:
Assign students daily practice playing this game at home turning the cards over to see whether the answers match.

KEY SIGNATURE CLUES

Objective:	Further develop a student's ability to quickly recognize key signatures
Student level:	Mid-Level I and Level II
Number of players:	Any number

Materials needed:
- A set of Key Signature flash cards

1. Arrange students in a semicircle. Hold the Key Signature flash cards in such a way that students cannot see the Key Signature or the answer on the back of the card.

2. Give a clue to the class about the card. For example, "I see a major key signature with five sharps. What is it?" The class answers, "B Major." Play continues with the next card.

Variations:
Gather the group into two teams. Give a clue to the first player in each line. Hand the flash card to the player who gives the correct answer. If both answer correctly, give both a card. If one player gives an incorrect answer, the other team's player can give the correct answer. Then both players move to the end of the line.

Late Level I and Level II: Reinforce recognition with clues for relative minor key signatures. Require players to answer the clue with both the major and the relative minor key.

KEY SIGNATURE TIC-TAC-TOE

Objective:	Further develop skills in writing and recognizing key signatures
Student level:	Mid-Level I and Level II with variations for Levels I, II and III
Number of players:	At least two players

Materials needed:
- Chalkboard or marker board with three sets of staff lines drawn on the board

1. Group the players into two teams: the "Treble Clefs" and the "Bass Clefs." The two teams line up facing the board.

2. Draw a tic-tac-toe matrix over the three sets of staff lines on the board. Each team member takes a turn naming a major key signature. The teacher writes the letter name of that key signature in the top left corner of the square designated by the student. See example below:

3. The Treble Clef team begins. The first player chooses a tic-tac-toe strategy as well as a square in which to write the key signature. If the center square is chosen (shown above as G), the student draws a treble clef, to show that the Treble Clef team occupies that square, and then fills in the designated key signature.

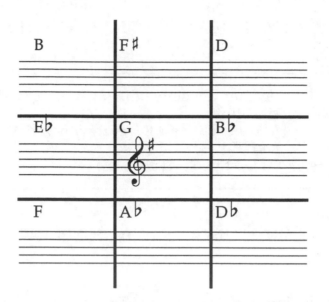

4. The other team watches and discusses the answer. If they decide that the Treble Clef team has written the key signature correctly, play continues. If the answer is written incorrectly, they erase both the key signature and the treble clef sign, and that square is again open to play. The next player, on the Bass Clef team, moves to the board and chooses an empty square in which to write his or her clef sign and key signature, and so forth.

5. As in a regular tic-tac-toe game, the team that gets three of the same clef signs in a row is the winner.

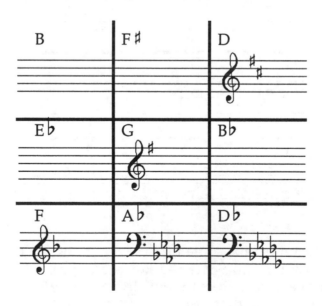

Variations:

Level I: The teacher writes a key signature in every square. The students, on each team, take turns writing the letter name of a key shown in the square they have chosen.

Level II and III: Write both major and minor letter names for key signatures on the matrix.

For other variations on Tic-Tac-Toe, see chapter 3 on lines and spaces recognition and chapter 6 on triads.

HOME REINFORCEMENT:

Assign daily practice with the Key Signature flash cards. A family member shows the cards to the student, and he or she names the key signatures as quickly as possible.

SCRAMBLED EGGS

Objective:	Reinforce the learning of key signatures
Student level:	Level I and Level II
Number of players:	Two or more

Materials needed:
- A one-dozen egg carton
- Twelve plastic eggs and a basket to hold them
- Twelve slips of paper, each with the number of flats or sharps corresponding to the 12 key signatures

1. Prior to class, the teacher cuts an egg carton in half and removes the lid. In the "wells" of each of the two bottom sections, he or she writes the letter name of a key signature.

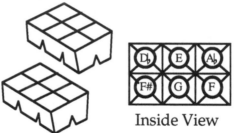

Inside View

Then the instructor cuts twelve pieces of construction paper and writes on each slip of paper one corresponding key signature with the number of sharps or flats on it.

The teacher slips one paper into each egg and places the eggs in the basket.

2. The instructor groups the class into two teams. Each team has an empty half carton in front of them, on a table or piano bench. Place the basket containing the 12 eggs within easy reach of both teams.

3. When the teacher says, "Start," the first student on each team reaches for an egg, opens it, and reads the slip inside. The students look to see if the number of sharps or flats shown on the paper corresponds with any of the letters in their half egg carton. For example, if the slip shows 2#'s the player looks for the letter D in the carton.

4. When the player finds the matching letter, the student re-places the paper in the egg, twists it together, and puts it in the correct place in the carton. He or she moves to the end of the line. If the student does not find the corresponding letter name in the carton, the slip of paper is re-placed in the egg and put back in the basket. The student moves to the end of the line and play continues.

5. If, by the end of play, there are eggs still remaining in the basket, it is an indication of mistakes. The teams unscrew each of the eggs placed in the cartons until they find and correct their mistakes.

Variations:
1. The teacher gives each member of the class a certain number of eggs. (A class of six students receives two eggs a piece.) When the instructor says "Start" the students quickly open their eggs and check the number of sharps or flats on the slips of paper. Then they twist the egg together and place it in the corresponding section of the egg carton.

2. Small groups of students can work together to see how quickly they can fill the carton.

3. Play this game in reverse by writing the number of sharps or flats in each key signature in the egg carton. Write the key signature letter name on the slips of paper.

HOME REINFORCEMENT:
Encourage students to memorize the number of flats and sharps in each key by playing the Key Signature Dice Game, outlined in this chapter, each day at home. They should refer to a picture showing the number of flats or sharps in each major key signature for help.

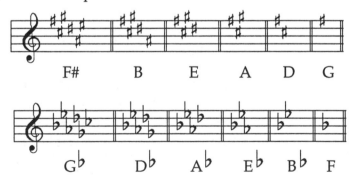

KEY SIGNATURE AND MINOR TRIAD MATCHING GAME

Objective:	Reinforce and simplify the learning of relative major key signatures
Student level:	Early Level II to Mid-Level II
Number of players:	At least four players

Materials needed:
- Two sets each of Minor Triads flash cards and Key Signature flash cards

Team 1   Team 2

1. The teacher groups the class into Team 1 and Team 2. Then the teacher places a set each of Minor Triads cards and Key Signature cards next to each other, on a table (or piano bench) for each team. Place the table approximately four to six feet away from the teams.

2. The first two students on each team listen for the instructor to say, "Start." These players take the top card off the set of Minor Triads cards and move over to the set of Key Signature cards, searching for the correct relative major key signature in either clef. The player finds the exact card, races back to their team and shows both cards to the teacher or to a student selected as checker. If the cards are correct, the student takes the cards and goes to the end of the line. Incorrect cards go on the bottom of the stack of flash cards.

Variations:
1. Before class the teacher removes one Minor Triads card, from the set, for each player. Then the student finds the matching relative major Key Signature card for each of the Minor Triads cards selected.

The teacher arranges the class into two teams and passes a Minor Triads card to each member of one team. Then the student gives a matching Key Signature card to each student on the other team. The instructor tells the students to hold their card in such a way that other players cannot see it until the game begins. When the teacher says "Start," the student with a Minor Triads card tries to find the student with the matching relative major Key Signature card. For example, a student with a C-Minor Triads card searches for a student holding an E-flat Major Key Signature card.

Partners with matching cards, step up to the board, where one student writes the minor triad and the other player writes the matching relative major key signature.

2. The instructor asks a student to spread out the set of Key Signature cards on the floor. The teacher hands one Minor Triads card to each student. When the instructor gives the signal, students see how quickly they can find the matching relative major Key Signature card. The teacher checks their cards and places the Minor Triads cards in the back of the stack. Place Key Signature cards back on the floor. Play continues with each student receiving a new Minor Triads card.

HOME REINFORCEMENT:
Students place their set of Minor Triads flash cards on the music rack of their piano, facing them. They play the card shown and then play immediately the relative major triad.

KEY SIGNATURE MATH

Objective:	Reinforce the learning of key signatures
Student level:	Late Level I and Level II with variations for Levels II, III and IV
Number of players:	Any number

Materials needed:
- Chalkboard or marker board

1. The teacher separates students into two teams facing the board. The instructor writes an equation, on the board, consisting of letters from major key signatures. For example:

F Major + E♭ Major = _____ (Answer: 4 flats)

D + B = _____ (Answer: 7 sharps)

2. The first two students at the front of the line rush to the board and write their answer. The teacher gives a point to the team with the correct answer. The instructor asks the other player, who had the wrong answer, to write the number of flats or sharps each letter receives. The player who wrote the correct answer assists. For example:

$$\begin{array}{cc} F & + & E♭ & = \underline{\hspace{2cm}} \\ 1 & & 3 \end{array}$$

Variations:

Write equations consisting of both flat and sharp keys (e.g., A♭ + E = 8).

Level II: Write equations that include both adding or subtraction
(e.g., A♭ - G = 3).

Levels III- IV: Write longer problems (e.g., A x B + G♭ = 21). Older students enjoy the challenge of equations mixing multiplication, division, addition, and subtraction.

HOME REINFORCEMENT:
Assign students to create three or four problems for their class, during the week, and bring them to the next lesson. Students try to stump their classmates with their equations.

CIRCLE-OF-FIFTHS RELAY

Objective:	Reinforce the learning of the circle of fifths and key signatures
Student level:	Late Level I with variations for Levels II, III, and IV
Number of players:	At least three players

Materials needed:
- Chalkboard or marker board
- Bean bag

Pre-game activity of Mental Gymnastics:
The students and the teacher (holding a bean bag) form a circle. The instructor starts the action by saying "I am C," then passes the bean bag to the student on her left, and asks, "Who are you?" That student responds "I am G," and turns to the left and passes the bean bag to the next player asking, "Who are you?" When students complete the "sharp" side of the circle of fifths by answering, "I am B. Who are you?" the next student answers, "I am F-sharp or G-flat." Play continues until they have said all of the letters in the circle of fifths. Play the game several times, each time starting with a different student.

Pre-game variation:
Level II, III, or IV: The teacher passes the bean bag to the student on his or her right and asks players to respond with the letters in the order of the circle of fourths.

RELAY RACE:
1. The teacher groups the class into two teams. The team captains are at the head of their lines facing the board.

2. When the instructor says, "Start," the team captains draw a large circle placing C at the top of their circle and write "0 flats or sharps" above it. When they are finished, they quickly pass their chalk or marker to the next player, who adds G and the one sharp.

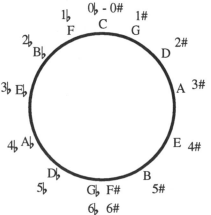

3. The game continues until students have written all the letters representing the circle of fifths and the corresponding number of flats and sharps, for each key.

4. The team who finishes first has their work checked by the opposing team.

Variations:
Circle of Fifths Olympics: Players work by themselves, at the board, to see how fast they can write the circle of fifths and the sharps and flats. Set a goal. Can they write it in less than a minute? The teacher posts the top time. The next week, students try to beat that time.

Levels II and III: Request that, in addition, students add the relative minors inside the circle. Players check themselves by drawing lines across the circle to like letters. For example, a student drawing a line from D Major to D-flat Major would show D Major, b minor and D-flat Major, b-flat minor.

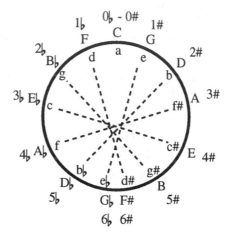

Levels III and IV: Ask students to write the circle of fourths, adding the relative minors on the inside of the circle.

HOME REINFORCEMENT:
Assign students to draw six circles on the back of their assignment sheet. (Suggest drawing their circle around a small drinking glass.) Each day they practice writing the circle of fifths and add the correct number of flats or sharps necessary for each key. Have the student indicate, under each circle, how many seconds or minutes it took them to complete the circle. Each day they work to better their time.

CIRCLE-OF-FIFTHS PARTNER CHALLENGE RACE

Objective:	Review the circle of fifths
Student level:	Level III and Level IV
Number of players:	Two players

Materials needed:
- One set of Major Triads flash cards
- One set of Minor Triads flash cards
- One set of Key Signature flash cards

Note: *Prior to playing the game, separate the Key Signature cards so that all treble cards are in one pile and all bass cards are in another pile.*

1. Hand one player a set of Major Triads flash cards. Instruct the student to place the triads, in either clef, on the floor in a four-to-five foot circle, to form the circle of fifths when the game begins. Seat the other student at the piano. Instruct this pupil to prepare to play a major and minor scale up and back (two or four octaves depending on their ability) and the cadence, in a specified key.

2. When the teacher says, "Start," the first student looks through the set of flash cards and quickly places the triads on the floor to form the circle of fifths. At the same time, challenge the pupil at the piano to play the scales and cadence before the other student can finish placing the triads.

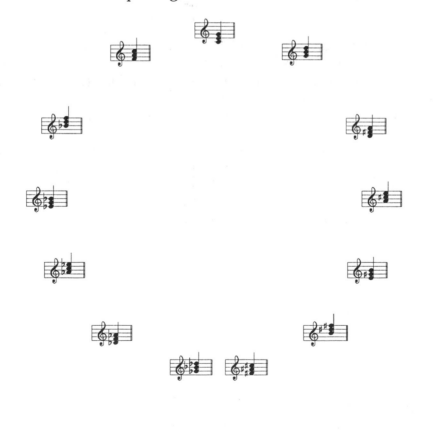

3. Now students switch places, and this time one pupil places the relative Minor Triads cards inside the circle, next to each of the Major Triads cards while the partner plays the scales and cadence, this time in a different specified key.

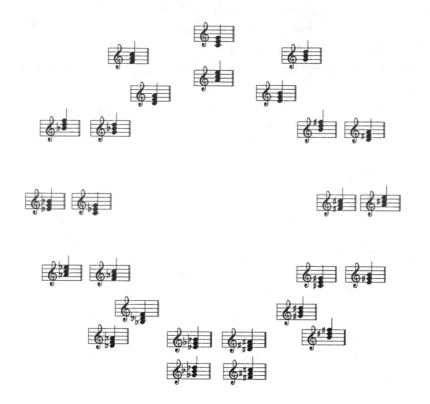

4. Now the teacher hands the treble Key Signature cards to one student and the bass cards to the partner. When the instructor says, "Start," the students place the correct Key Signature card, on the outside of the circle, next to the corresponding triad. Students can only place one Key Signature card next to the triads. The object is to see which student can place more Key Signature cards around the circle.

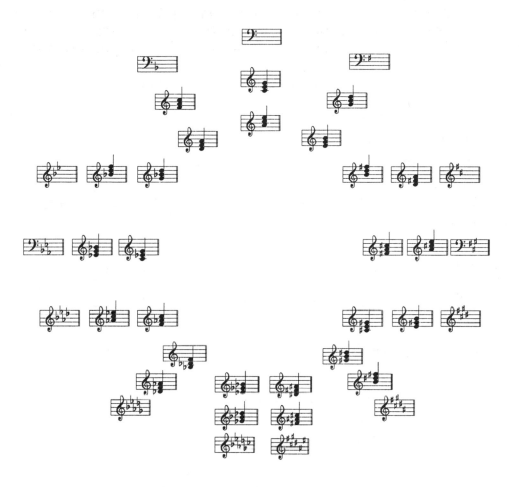

HOME REINFORCEMENT:
The week prior to playing the "Circle-of-Fifths Partner Challenge Race," assign students to draw six circles on the back of their assignment sheet. (Suggest drawing their circle around a small drinking glass.) Each day they practice writing the circle of fifths and add the correct number of flats or sharps necessary for each key. Inside the circle instruct them to write the names of the relative minors.

KEY SIGNATURE UPSET

Objective:	Reinforce the association of key signatures with the number of flats or sharps in each corresponding key
Student level:	Level II
Number of players:	Six or more

Materials needed:
- Two sets of fifteen 2" x 3" cards with just the letter name of a key signature marked on each one, as shown below

Note: *A large playing area is recommended.*

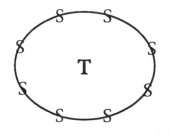

1. The players stand in a large circle, and the teacher distributes all the cards to them. The teacher is "It" and stands in the middle of the circle. Players check their cards to make sure they do not have two cards with letters alike. If anyone does, the teacher takes one and switches it with a card from another player.

2. The teacher starts the game by calling out a key signature – for example, "five sharps." The two students who have the cards with the letter B on them look at the students around the circle, secretly signaling that they have the cards. When the two students with the B cards make eye contact, they step forward and try to quickly exchange places before the teacher can get into one of their places. If the teacher gets into one of their spots before the two students exchange places, the student without a place becomes "It." The teacher takes the student's cards and stands with the other players in the circle.

3. Sometimes a student holds the letter called for but has forgotten the name of the key. The player holding the matching card steps forward, looking around for someone to exchange places with. At this point, the teacher asks who has the matching card. The player who held the identical card but did not change places becomes "It." The student who was "It" now takes that player's cards and returns to the circle.

4. Occasionally, call "Key Signature Upset." All students in the circle quickly exchange places. "It" attempts to get into any other player's place and force that player into the center of the circle. The player in the center is now "It."

Variation:
Make another double set of fifteen cards. This time write the number of flats or sharps for each key signature, as shown below.

1♭	1#	2♭'s	2#'s	3♭'s	3#'s	4♭'s	4#'s	5♭'s	5#'s	6♭'s	6#'s	7♭'s	7#'s	0♭'s 0#'s

All rules from the above-mentioned game apply, except now the player that is "It," in the center of the circle, calls the letter name of the key signature – for example, "D-flat." The two players who are holding cards with five flats written on them must try to exchange places.

Since this game takes longer to play than some of the other games, you may wish to save it for special occasions.

For other variations on this game, see chapter 3 on lines and spaces recognition and chapter 6 on triads.

Chapter Note: *Students who are taught to listen with concentration will achieve greater success with their music and with reading and spelling activities, where listening skills are also necessary.*

RHYTHM READING CARDS

Objective:	Strengthen rhythmic skills and make the association of short and long rhythmic dashes with actual note values
Student level:	Very young beginners and Level I
Number of players:	At least two

Materials needed:
- Four long-and-short-rhythm cards (approximately 4" x 9") with the four basic rhythms drawn in dashes, as shown below:

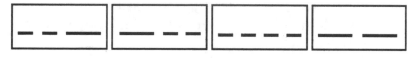

- Four note value cards, with the matching note values drawn on them, as shown below:

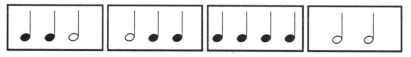

1. The students sit on the floor, in a semicircle, facing the instructor. Place the set of long-and-short-rhythm cards in a row on the floor. The students read, clap, and verbalize (e.g., "short, short, l-o-n-g") the short and long patterns on the cards as the teacher points to the various rhythms.

2. Ask a student to mix the cards and to place them in a new pattern. The student then points to the cards as the class reads, claps, and verbalizes the rhythms.

3. The teacher sends the students to the board and assigns some to be writers while others act as helpers. They all listen for the teacher to play a rhythm from one card. Facing the teacher, they clap the rhythm they have heard, then turn and write it in dashes on the board. The helper assists in writing the correct rhythm. Next, the helper and writer switch places so that everyone gets a turn to write. As students gain skill, the teacher can play the rhythms on two or more cards.

Variations:

1. After introducing note values, mix the long-and-short-rhythm cards with the note value cards and place them on the floor. Group students as partners. Give each set of partners a chance to match the rhythm cards to the note value cards. The other students check for accuracy while they await their turn.

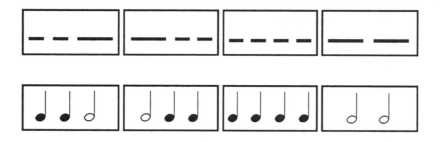

2. Group students as partners. Then seat them on the floor. Cut out, ahead of time, eight short pieces and four long pieces of construction paper for each set of partners. The teacher plays a rhythm and the partners clap it back and place their slips of paper in the correct order.

Note: *You may substitute two sizes of wooden blocks for the construction paper.*

RHYTHMIC DICE

Objective:	Strengthen student's ability to recognize note values
Student level:	Very young beginners and Level I
Number of players:	Any number

Materials needed:
- Two plain dice.

Using a permanent marker draw one of the following notes on each side of the dice.

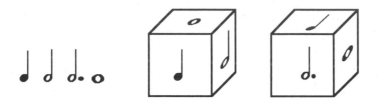

Then repeat any two of the notes so all six sides of the dice show a note value.

1. The teacher rolls the two dice to the students seated on the floor in a semicircle. They answer by saying the note names and values shown on the two dice. They then give the sum of the two dice added together.

2. Very young children can hold up the correct number of fingers to indicate the value shown on the dice. For example, if the die rolled on the left showed a quarter note, the students would hold up one finger on their left hand. Should a whole note appear on the die on the right, students would hold up four fingers on their right hand. The pupils count their fingers to arrive at the sum.

Variations:
1. Add the eighth note and two eighth notes to the dice.

2. Write rests on all sides of one die. Students roll this die and a die with note values on it.

3. Make a game board using poster board and address labels. Arrange the labels in any pattern you choose. Decorate the board with musical stickers. For game pieces, use colored papers, buttons, or markers from other games. Using a single die, students take turns rolling and moving their marker according to the value of the note shown on the die.

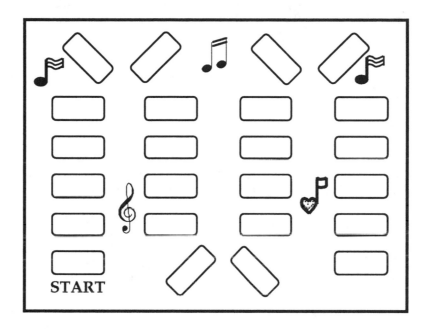

SHAPE CARD EAR TRAINING

Objective:	Sharpen listening skills and enable students to easily distinguish between root, third, and fifth
Student level:	Very young beginners and Level I with variations for Early Level I and Mid-Level I
Number of players:	Any number

Materials needed:
- At least six 3" x 5" cards and a pack of plain round stickers

The teacher makes a set of shape cards by placing dots on the cards to represent the root, third, and fifth (low, middle, high) of the scale.

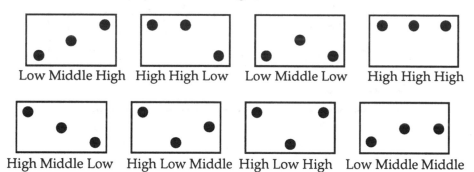

Low Middle High   High High Low   Low Middle Low   High High High

High Middle Low   High Low Middle   High Low High   Low Middle Middle

1. The students stand in a semicircle facing the teacher. The instructor holds the shape cards so the class can see them. The students read, verbalize (e.g., "high, low, middle") and body-shape each card by reaching to their toes for low, waist for middle, and head for high. Cards may be turned upside down to create new patterns.

2. Give each student six or eight 3" x 5" cards and a sheet of stickers. Ask each student to name a pattern (i.e., a pattern combining low, middle, and high). The class place their stickers on their cards to correspond with the pattern named. Students enjoy seeing how many different patterns of *low, middle, high* combinations they can think of and like to make their own set of cards to work with at home.

3. The teacher spreads four to six shape cards out along the music rack. The class listens while the teacher plays the shape shown on one of the cards. The instructor asks a pupil to go to the piano and pick out the card played.

Variations:

1. Place four shape cards on the music rack and direct a student to play them in the order shown. That pupil then rearranges the cards for another student to play.

2. The students form a line facing the piano. The teacher tells the class the key and asks them to look away as he or she plays one of the *low, middle, high* patterns on the piano. All students listen and body-shape the pattern, and the person at the front of the line moves to the piano and plays the shape heard. The teacher asks the class if they heard the correct shape played. Should the student play incorrectly, the teacher repeats the pattern and the student tries again. The pupil goes to the end of the line after playing the pattern accurately. Play continues with a new pattern for the next student.

3. Group students as partners and send them to the board. Some students are writers and some are helpers. The writers draw a treble and a bass clef. The teacher gives the name of the key and plays a *low, middle, high* pattern. The pupils point to the staff indicating the lines or spaces that *low, middle, high* fall on in the specified key.

Note: *When working with young children, direct them to write "L" for low, "M" for middle, and "H" for high in the correct places on the staff to indicate the perimeter they will work within.*

The instructor plays any low, middle, high pattern on the piano. The students body-shape the pattern they hear and then, using slashes for quick melodic dictation, write the shape played. Partners then switch places so each has a turn to write.

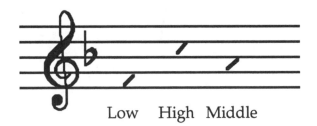

Low   High   Middle

4 When students are successful with three tones, add four, and so on.

5. Add rhythms to the *low, middle, high* patterns. Students write these rhythms at the board or use small blocks of wood or heavy paper cut into short and long strips, laying them out vertically or horizontally on the floor to correspond with the shape and rhythmic pattern played.

HOME REINFORCEMENT:
Very young beginners and Early Level I: Send a set of shape cards home with each of the students. Assign them to place the cards on the music rack and play each of the shapes on the cards. For additional shapes, remind pupils to turn the cards upside down. Each day play the shape cards in a different key.

Early Level I: Instruct students to use the shape cards to make variations by changing the first three notes of their pieces with a shape shown on one of their cards. Play a different variation for every shape card. The next day turn the cards over and create new variations.

Mid-Level I: Instruct students to place four shape cards on the music rack to reinforce Question and Answers. The student plays the "shapes" shown on the four cards and then creates an Answer. The pupil rearranges the cards to form a new Question to answer.

RHYTHMIC SONG PUZZLE

Objective:	Mentally visualize and reinforce rhythmic patterns within a song
Student level:	Very young beginners and Level I
Number of players:	At least two

Materials needed:
- Several sets of eight 3" x 6" pieces of construction paper

Each piece of paper will represent one measure each of a short song the students are working on. Write the rhythm on the cards. Make one set of rhythm cards for each team of players. Take, for example, the eight measures from the piece "Old Woman" which are shown below:

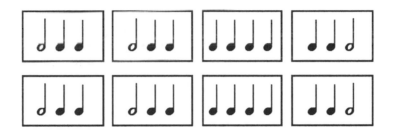

1. Review a song, such as "Old Woman," first by clapping and verbalizing the rhythm (half note, quarter, quarter, and so on.) Ask a student to play the piece on the piano.

2. Group the class into teams of two to four students each. Mix each set of eight cards and spread them out on the floor, face up, in front of each team. When the teacher says, "Start," each team tries to quickly find and place their cards in the proper rhythmic order of the song.

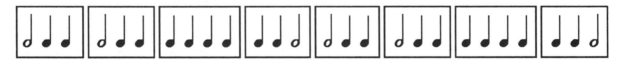

3. Once a team finishes placing its cards in order, the teacher asks everyone to stop and clap the rhythm to see if it is correct. If the rhythm is incorrect, the team goes back to work and tries to complete the song before another group does.

Variation:
Play the game with two familiar songs. The teacher tells each team secretly which song they have and hands them those rhythm cards. The teams quickly place their cards in the correct order of the song. Team A claps the rhythm seen on team B's cards and tries to guess the name of their song. Team B then claps the rhythm on team A's cards and tries to guess their piece.

IDENTIFYING INTERVALS

Objective:	Develop interval awareness
Student level:	Level I with variations for Level II
Number of players:	Five or more

Materials needed:
- Chalkboard or marker board or pencil and paper

1. Arrange five students either sitting or standing in a row. Number each pupil from one to five, representing the five tones of the scale.

2. The teacher plays the root and a third above it. Student one and student three raise their hands, and so on. The teacher always starts with the root tone.

3. As reinforcement at the board, students write numbers one through five diagonally on the board or on paper.

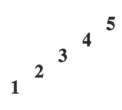

As the teacher plays an interval, students point or draw a line to the correct number for the interval played. For example, if the teacher plays a fourth, the students draw a line from 1 to 4, like so:

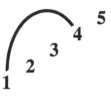

Variations (Late Level I and Level II):
1. With more advanced students, use all eight tones.

2. Ask students to quickly identify what they hear. See examples below:
   - The teacher plays skips and steps. The class verbalizes the answers.
   - The instructor plays various intervals. Students show the intervals heard with upraised fingers.
   - The teacher plays major and minor triads. Students show a major triad with an open upraised hand and a minor triad with their hand closed.
   - I and V7 chords are indicated with upraised fingers – one finger to indicate the I chords and five fingers to indicate the V7 chords.

3. Students listen to the chords the teacher uses to accompany a melodic line. They verbalize and show the number of the chord with upraised fingers or by writing the Roman numerals quickly on the board.

4. As the teacher plays a simple song, students anticipate the chords the teacher will play to accompany the melody, naming the chord just before the teacher plays it.

BASKETBALL
Single-Note Listening Game

Objective:	Reinforce skills in the hearing of intervals
Student level:	Young beginners through Level III
Number of players:	Two or more

Materials needed:
- None

1. Group the students into two teams facing one of the piano keyboards. The teacher is at the second piano. If only one keyboard is available, the teacher shields what he or she is playing with the other hand so that students cannot observe what is being played.

2. The teacher instructs students to look away while he or she plays middle C, then the C an octave above it, and then any white note between the two C's.

3. The first student, on team 1, plays the two C's, which are the perimeter of the basketball court, and then tries to match the third tone played by the teacher.

4. If the student plays the three tones correctly the first time, the team receives two points. If the student misses, the teacher turns to the other students and asks if the third tone played was too high or too low. The student then receives another turn and listens carefully while the teacher plays the same three tones again. If the pupil is successful, the team gets one point. Allow only two tries.

5. The player moves to the end of the line and play continues with a member from team 2.

Variations:
1. When students have mastered playing the third tone on any given white key within the octave, play the third tone on a black key.

2. Then play the third tone on either a black or white key within the octave.

3. This activity can be expanded by playing the two perimeter keys first and then either a white or black key within two, then three, and eventually four octaves.

HOME REINFORCEMENT: Students will find this a fun activity to practice at home with a family member.

EAR TRAINING WITH KEY SIGNATURES

Objective:	Strengthen the student's ability to hear intervals and reinforce the learning of key signatures
Student level:	Level I
Number of players:	Any number

Materials needed:
- Chalkboard or marker board
- Key Signature flash cards
- Floor staff
- A set of seven large cards (approximately 8" x 9") with one letter of the musical alphabet written on each card

$$\boxed{A} \quad \boxed{B} \quad \boxed{C} \quad \boxed{D} \quad \boxed{E} \quad \boxed{F} \quad \boxed{G}$$

1. The teacher prepares the seven letter cards and gives one to each player.

2. Students listen to and shape the intervals in the air with their fingers as the instructor plays the first six flats on the piano as follows: starting with B-flat, going up to E-flat, down to A-flat, up to D-flat, down to G-flat, and up to C-flat. The class recognizes these intervals as the flat pattern.

3. The teacher reviews the sharp patterns, playing the first six sharps, as follows: starting with F-sharp, going down to C-sharp, up to G-sharp, down to D-sharp, down to A-sharp, and up to E-sharp.

4. The teacher plays the sharps or flats in one of the key signatures on the piano. For example, for the key of A-flat, the teacher plays the first four flats of the key signature, as follows: starting with B-flat, going up to E-flat, down to A-flat, and up to D-flat. Students holding the letter cards that match these notes quickly arrange themselves on the floor staff in the pattern of the key signature they just heard. Players hold their card in front of them so the rest of the class can check that they are standing in the right place.

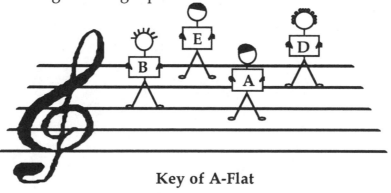

Key of A-Flat

To indicate that they are sharps, students raise one hand in the air. To indicate flats, they put one hand on their shoulder. As shown below.

Sharp   Flat

Variations:
1. The teacher spreads a set of Key Signature flash cards on the floor and the players form a circle around the cards. The teacher plays a key signature pattern on the piano. Players listen and then quickly try to find the correct Key Signature card.

2. The students step up to the board in pairs. The teacher asks one person to write and the other student to help. The teacher will play the sharps or flats of a key signature on the piano, and the students will write the key signature pattern on the board. For example, the teacher plays the first three sharps of the sharp key signature, and the students write the A-Major key signature pattern on the board. The helpers check and make any needed corrections. Helpers switch roles with writers and listen to the next key signature the teacher plays.

HOME REINFORCEMENT:
Students place their Key Signature flash cards face up on the music rack of the piano. They play the sharps or flats in the order shown on each card and listen to the intervals. For example, a D-Major key signature shown in bass clef would be played on F-sharp, and then down to C-sharp, in the octave below middle C.

SELF-DICTATION

Objective:	Further develop ear training skills through daily practice at home
Student level:	Late Level I through Advanced
Number of players:	Any number

Materials needed:
• Staff paper and pencil

1. Instruct students to take one or two consecutive measures of melodic or rhythmic dictation from an assigned piece of music.

2. Instruct them to:
• Carefully study the chosen measures.
• Clap the rhythm.
• Play the measures.
• Shut the book.
• Write what they remember.
• Open the book and check what they have written.

3. Ask them to bring their staff book to the next lesson to be checked.

Students who are having difficulty memorizing certain parts of a piece will find this activity beneficial.

HOME REINFORCEMENT:
Instruct students to take one or two consecutive measures of melodic or rhythmic dictation each day at home from an assigned piece of music.

QUESTION-AND-ANSWER DICTATION

Objective:	Strengthen ear training and creative skills
Student level:	Level III, Level IV, and Level V
Number of players:	Any number

Materials needed:
- Chalkboard or marker board or staff paper

1. The teacher instructs the students to write a treble clef, a bass clef, and a specified key signature.

2. Students listen to the four-measure question played by their teacher. Then they write either a parallel or contrasting answer in the style of the question.

3. When students have completed writing their answers, the teacher plays the question again for each pupil. The students take turns responding on the keyboard with their answer.

ADVANCED DICTATION

Objective: Develop acute ear training skills
Student level: Level IV and Level V
Number of players: Any number

Materials needed:
  • Chalkboard, marker board, or staff paper

1. Four students go to the board (or use staff paper). Assign each student one specific measure of the piece to take dictation on.

2. The first student on the left writes the treble clef, the bass clef, and the designated key signature. He or she allows room to write the first measure and draws a bar line. The other pupils divide their place at the board with a bar line.

3. The teacher plays four measures of music. Each person in the group listens carefully for the measure they will write. The instructor repeats the music again and each student writes their assigned measure.

4. The teacher then plays what the students have written. Pupils make corrections as needed.

CHORD SETS MATCH-UP ACTIVITY

Objective:	Simplify the learning of chords by grouping them according to their arrangement of white and black keys
Student level:	Level I
Number of players:	Two to eight

Materials needed:
- Major Triads flash cards

1. After introducing the students to the four Chord Sets, as shown below, gather the class into groups of two to four pupils each. Each group should have a complete set of Major Triads cards.

2. Instruct each group to remove from their set the four cards with three chords on them representing the Chord Sets in either clef. Have students lay them on the floor, one below the other. Allow plenty of space between each group of players so those students setting out their cards don't overlap the cards laid out by the other team.

 Chords that are in the "All White Set"

 Chords in the "Black In The Middle Set"

 Chords in the "White In The Middle Set"

The "Odd Set"

3. Players sort through their set of cards, finding and matching all of the chords in each Chord Set. Instruct the players to place the matching cards to the right of each Chord Set card. For instance, a card showing a D-Major chord is placed next to the Chord Set card that has a D chord in it.

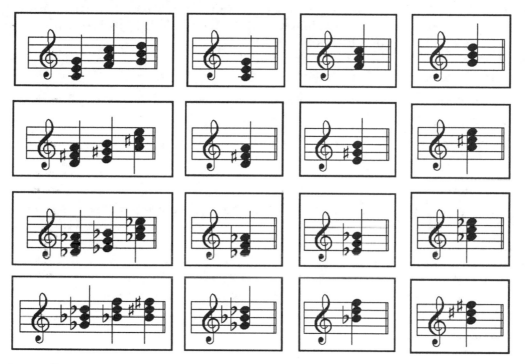

4. A small group of two to four students could lay out both treble and bass cards beside their Chord Set cards.

5. Gather a larger class into four groups, and use two sets of Major Triads cards. Give group A and group B one set of cards to spread out on the floor or table. Group A will find and lay out just treble-clef cards, next to their Chord Set cards, while group B only lays out bass-clef cards. Group C and group D would do the same thing in another large area of the room.

The object is to see how quickly one can find the matching chords for each of the Chord Set cards.

HOME REINFORCEMENT:
1. Students can practice arranging these cards at home, perhaps timing themselves to see how quickly they can match the triads to the Chord sets.

2. Play the game with a parent, brother, or sister.

3. Take the cards to the keyboard and play the chords in their correct places.

CHORD SET MENTAL GYMNASTICS

Objective:	Mentally picture and identify chords in four groupings: All White, Black in the Middle, White in the Middle, and The Odd Set
Student level:	Mid-Level I and Level II
Number of players:	Any number

Materials needed:
  • Chalkboard or marker board with staff lines drawn on the board

 Chords that are in the "All White Set"

 Chords in the "Black In The Middle Set"

 Chords in the "White In The Middle Set"

 The "Odd Set"

1. Group students into teams or have them work in pairs at the board (one student writing, the other helping). As soon as students have drawn a treble clef and a bass clef, the teacher asks them to write a missing chord from a Chord Set. For instance the teacher might say, "I am thinking of two chords from a Chord Set. They are G-flat and B. Write the missing chord in that set." The players quickly write the B-flat chord in both treble and bass clefs and turn around to face the other students, who check their work.

2. The first student to write the correct chord gets a point for his or her team. Both players move to the end of the line, and play continues.

3. When the class is proficient at writing the one missing chord, change your statement and say to the group: "I am thinking of a Chord Set that has an F chord in it. Write the other two chords in that Set." The correct answer is the C and G chord.

HOME REINFORCEMENT:
1. Assign the writing of the Chord Sets on staff paper.

2. The student asks a family member to quiz them on the chords in the various sets.

3. Using the Major Triads flash cards, students find the individual chords for each set.

BUILDING TRIADS

Objective:	Reinforce the structure of triads for easy recognition
Student level:	Level I with variations for Levels II and III
Number of players:	Four or more

Materials needed:

- A set each of Major Triads cards and Chromatic Flash cards

- Three white and three black 2" x 2" cards

- A set of seven small cards (approximately 2" x 5") with one letter of the musical alphabet written on each card

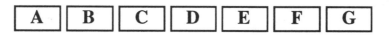

- Three cards with a sharp on each card and three cards with a flat on each card

♯	♯	♯	♭	♭	♭

1. Group the students into four "stations." Give each group a different set of cards to work with at their station.

Station 1 takes the Chromatic flash cards and spreads them out, facing up, on the floor or table.

Station 2 takes the Major Triads cards and spreads them out also, facing up, on the floor or table.

Station 3 separates their black and white cards

Station 4 separates their letter cards from their sharp and flat cards.

When all stations have prepared their cards, play is ready to begin.

2. The teacher calls out a major triad – for example, "D Major:"

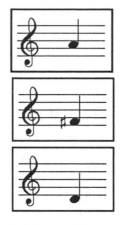

Station 1 hunts through the Chromatic cards and finds the three notes necessary to spell the D triad. Students place their cards one above the other in the proper order.

Station 2 looks through the Major Triads cards for the D triad.

Station 3 selects their black and white pattern to match the triad called for. For a D-Major triad, students arrange the cards in white, black, white order.

Station 4 spells their triad with letters and places the correct accidental beside their letter card.

3. When all four groups have finished laying their cards out, the teacher and students check to see that all groups match each other.

4. Each group then rotates to the next station, giving them a turn at each activity.

For a large group, add two more stations by dividing the two groups with flash cards into treble and bass teams. These groups look for cards in the clef assigned them.

Variations:
Level II: Use Minor Triads and Diminished Triads flash cards to replace the Major Triads.

Level III: Use Augmented Triads flash cards to replace the Major Triads flash cards.

HOME REINFORCEMENT:
1. Students spread out their Chromatic flash cards, facing up, on the floor in front of them. A parent, older brother or sister, or baby-sitter could call out a triad. The student quickly picks out the correct notes on the flash cards to spell the triad.

2. Students can call out their own triads and find the cards that spell them.

TRIAD TIC-TAC-TOE

Objective:	Develop skills in recognizing and writing triads
Student level:	Level I with variations for Levels II, III, and IV
Number of players:	Two or more

Materials needed:
- Chalkboard or marker board with three sets of staff lines drawn on the board

1. Group the players into two teams called the "Treble Clefs" and the "Bass Clefs." The two teams line up facing the board.

2. Draw a tic-tac-toe matrix over the three sets of staff lines on the board. Each team member takes a turn naming a major triad. The teacher writes the letter name in the top left corner of the square designated by the student. See example below:

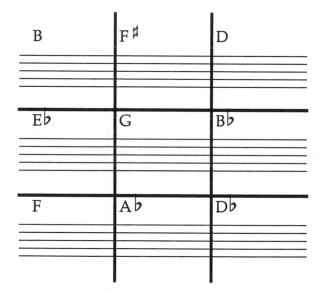

3. The Treble Clef team begins. The first player chooses a tic-tac-toe strategy as well as a square in which to write the indicated triad. The player draws a treble clef sign in the chosen square to show that the Treble Clef team occupies that square, and then writes in the triad.

Note: *When first introduced to the game, students may want to reinforce triad writing by silently playing the triad on the piano before writing it on the board.*

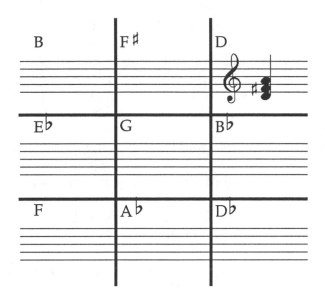

4. The other team watches and discuss the answer. If they decide that the Treble Clef team has written the triad correctly, play continues. If the answer is written incorrectly, they erase the incorrect answer and the treble clef sign, and that square is again open to play. The next player, on the Bass Clef team, moves to the board and chooses an empty square in which to write his or her clef sign and triad, and so forth.

5. As in the regular tic-tac-toe game, the team that gets three treble or three bass clef signs in a row is the winner.

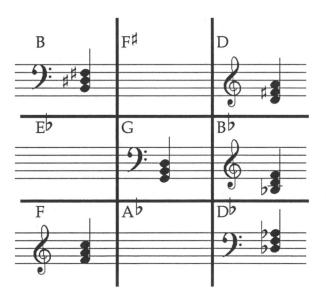

Variations:
Start with a plain matrix drawn over three sets of staff lines. A player from the Treble Clef team draws a triad in the square of his or her choice. Then a player from the Bass Clef team must name the triad. If the answer is correct, they erase the triad and write in the Treble or the Bass Clef sign for their team. Three Treble or Bass Clef signs in a row make their team the winner.

Level II: Add minor, diminished and I, IV, V7 triads to this game.

Level III: Add augmented and inverted triads at this level.

Level IV: Play the game using seventh chords or have students write the IIx7 chord (dominant of the dominant) in the given keys shown on the matrix.

Look for additional variations in chapters 3 on lines and spaces recognition and chapter 4 on key signatures.

Note: *This game, which has unlimited applications, is a favorite activity.*

PLAYING MINOR AND RELATIVE MAJOR TRIADS

Objective:	Relate minor and relative major triads and their key signatures
Student level:	Mid-Level I and Level II
Number of players:	Any number

Materials needed:
- Set of Major Triads flash cards
- Set of Minor Triads flash cards
- A board with two sets of staff lines

Group the class into two lines facing the piano keyboard.

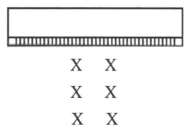

Place a Minor Triads flash card on the music rack of the piano and ask the student in line one to quickly play that minor triad and then the relative major triad. If the player plays the two triads correctly, he or she takes the card and moves to the end of the line. Should both teams miss, play reverts to the next person on team one.

Variations:
1. The two groups line up facing the chalkboard. The teacher shows a Minor Triads flash card to the first two students in line and asks them to go to the board and write the correct relative major key signature. Other players observe and check for accuracy what is being written. If the answers are correct, the first two students step to the end of the line. If the answers are incorrect, the class helps to correct them.

2. Show a Minor Triads card and ask students to write the relative or parallel major triad. Again, if students write the correct answer, they move to the end of the line. If the answer is incorrect, the class helps the student rectify the problem.

3. Display a Major Triads card and have students write the relative or parallel minor triad.

4. Show a Minor Triads card to the next players at the board, asking them to write either the parallel or relative major key signature.

HOME REINFORCEMENT:
Students place the Minor Triads flash cards on the piano and go through the set, playing the triad shown on the card, and then the relative major of each triad.

TRIAD SPELL

Objective:	Help students quickly recognize triads
Student level:	Mid-Level I with variations for Late Level I, Mid-Level II, and Level III
Number of players:	At least three

Materials needed:
- Bean bag

1. Students stand in a semicircle facing the teacher. The teacher gently tosses a bean bag to the first student on the left and asks that player to spell a certain major triad. The student catches the bean bag and immediately throws it back (to the teacher), spelling the letters of the triad called for. Give each player just one chance to answer each time it is their turn.

2. If the spelling is correct, the bean bag is tossed to the next person in the semicircle, and the spelling of a new triad is asked for.

3. However, if the player spells the triad incorrectly, the teacher tosses the bean bag to the next person in the semicircle asking that student to spell the same triad.

4. A student who does not know the answer tosses the bean bag right back to the teacher. The instructor then tosses the bean bag to the next player and asks for the same triad.

Play continues until all students have had a least one turn.

Variations:
1. The teacher, facing the students in a semicircle, holds a Key Signature flash card and asks the first student to spell a major triad built on the root of the key shown on the card.

2. Gather the students into three teams facing the teacher. The teacher calls out "G-Major triad". The first student in line #1 says the root of the triad (G). The student in line #2 answers with the third of the triad (B). The student at the beginning of line #3 calls out the fifth of the triad (D). Toss the bean bag to each player prior to having them give their answer. The other players listen and decide if the answers are correct. Students who answer accurately move to the end of the line.

Late Level I: Include V7 triads and minor triads.

Mid-Level II: Add diminished triads and the IV chord to the activity.

Level III: Add inversions to the game and, later, the augmented triads. Mix major, minor, diminished and augmented triads.

HOME REINFORCEMENT:
1. Instruct students to spell their arpeggios as they play them each day.

2. Have students place the set of Major Triads flash cards on their piano music rack. Suggest that they practice playing each triad, spelling it as they play it.

CHORD CLUES

Objective:	Sharpen chord recognition skills
Student level:	Late Level I with variations for Levels II, III and IV
Number of players:	Any number

Materials needed:
  • A set of Chromatic flash cards

1. Students sit in a semicircle facing the teacher. Hold the flash cards in such a way that students cannot see the answer on the back of the card. The teacher decides if the students are to answer all at once or individually.

2. A player (or the class) listens to the clue the teacher gives about the note seen on the top card of the set of flash cards. See the examples below:

> "This note is in treble clef second space and is the top of what major chord?" The player answers, "D Major."

> "I see a note that has a flat beside it on bass clef second line. This note is the middle of what minor chord?" The player answers, "G minor."

Variations:
Group the class into two lines facing the teacher. The first player on each team tries to answer before the student on the other team does. Allow players only one chance to answer. The team member getting the correct answer takes the card, and both players move to the end of the line. If members of both teams give the wrong answer, repeat the clue to the next two players.

Level II: Add clues for Diminished Triads flash cards.

Level III: Include Augmented Triads flash cards.

Level IV: Give clues for the top tone of the seventh chords.

HOME REINFORCEMENT:
Students place their set of Chromatic flash cards facing them on the music rack of their piano.

1. One day they practice playing a triad that uses the note they see as the <u>middle</u> note of the chord.

2. The next day, the note they see on each card will be the <u>top</u> note of the triad that they play, and so on.

3. Assign students to work out clues at home and bring them to the next lesson.

TRIAD UPSET

Objective:	Strengthen the student's ability to quickly think triads	
Student level:	Mid-Level II and Level III	
Number of players:	Six or more	

Materials needed:
- Two sets of 15 small cards (approximately 2" x 3") with a letter of the musical alphabet written on each card, as shown below.

Note: *You will need a large area to play this game.*

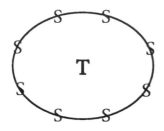

1. The players stand in a large circle, and the teacher distributes all the cards to them. The teacher is "It" and stands in the middle of the circle. Players check their cards to make sure they do not have two cards with letters alike. If anyone does, the teacher takes one and switches it with a card from another player.

2. The teacher starts the game by calling out the middle or top note of a major, or minor triad. If the teacher calls out "the middle note of an F-Major triad," the two students who have the cards with the letter A on them look at the students around the circle, secretly signaling that they have the cards. When the two students with the A cards make eye contact, they step forward and try to quickly exchange places before the teacher can get into one of their places. If the teacher gets into one of their spots before the two students exchange places, the student without a place becomes "It." The teacher takes the student's cards and stands with the other players in the circle.

3. Sometimes a student holds the letter called for, but has forgotten how to spell a triad and does not move. The player, holding the matching card steps forward, looking around for someone to exchange places with. At this point, the teacher asks who has the matching card. The player who held the identical card but did not change places becomes "It." The student who had been "It" now takes that player's cards and returns to the circle.

4. Occasionally call "Triad Upset." All students in the circle quickly exchange places. "It" attempts to get into any other player's place and force that player into the center of the circle. The player in the center is now "It."

Since this game takes longer to play than some of the other games, you may wish to save it for special occasions.

For other variations on this game see chapter 3 on lines and spaces recognition and chapter 4 on key signatures.

HOME REINFORCEMENT:
Level I: Assign daily practice in spelling major and minor arpeggios as students play them.

Early Level II: Assign daily practice in broken diminished triads by having students spell them as they play them in all keys.

Level III: Assign students to spell broken augmented triads as they play them in every key.

ADVANCED MENTAL GYMNASTICS

Objective:	Challenge advanced students as they review previously taught musical fundamentals
Student level:	Level IV and Level V
Number of players:	Any number

Materials needed:
- Chalkboard or marker board
- Key Signature flash cards

1. Group students as partners and send them to the board.

2. The teacher challenges the class with previously worked out problems. For example, the teacher asks them to write the triads that are the answers to the following problems:

> In the major key with five sharps, write the chord built on the seventh degree of the scale in its second inversion.

> In the major key with three flats, write the chord built on the third degree of the scale in its first inversion.

> "A major third above F is a perfect fifth above the top of what augmented triad?" Students write a D-flat triad.

> "A minor third above C is the top of what dominant seventh chord?" Students write an F7 chord.

> Show a major Key Signature flash card and ask the class to write the IIx7 (dominant of the dominant) chord in the key shown.

HOME REINFORCEMENT:
The students work on one or two problems of their own at home and bring them to challenge the group the next week.